THE MARITAL ARTS

ALSO BY ARTHUR HOPPE

The Love Everybody Crusade

Dreamboat

The Perfect Solution to Absolutely Everything

Mr. Nixon and My Other Problems

Miss Lollipop and the Doom Machine

The Tiddling Tennis Theorem

THE MARITAL ARTS

ARTHUR HOPPE

ARBOR HOUSE | *NEW YORK*

Manufactured in the United States of America

10 9 8 7 6 5 4 3 2 1

This book is printed on acid free paper. The paper in
this book meets the guidelines for permanence and
durability of the Committee on Production Guidelines
for Book Longevity of the Council on Library Resources.

Library of Congress Cataloging in Publication Data

Hoppe, Arthur Watterson.
  The marital arts.

  1.Marriage—Anecdotes, facetiae, satire, etc.
I. Title.
PS3558.O6368M3   1985   814'.54   85-3878
ISBN 0-87795-676-6 (alk. paper)

I recently wrote a book on sex which didn't sell too well. "Why don't you write a book on a subject you know something about?" suggested my dear wife helpfully. The result is this book on marriage which I lovingly dedicate to my dear wife, whose name is not Glynda, and to the other six people who made it possible, my four children, whose names are not Mordred and Malphasia, and my two friends and editors, whose names are Janice Greene and Stanleigh Arnold.

I should mention that the invaluable advice set forth herein has been culled from the more than five thousand daily newspaper columns, as well as assorted magazine articles and books, that I have ground out over the years. It comprises all I know about marriage and all, as I look at it, that anyone needs to know.

CONTENTS

PART 1: MARRIAGE

Contents

PART TWO: THE FAMILY

THE MARITAL ARTS

MARRIAGE

I've been married for nigh on thirty-two years and I don't regret one, single, solitary day of it. The one, single, solitary day of it I don't regret is May 16, 1873. I forget why.

—The Wit and Wisdom of Joshua Xavier Sneckle, 1884

CHAPTER ONE

Marriage: A Challenge for the Eighties

I HAD STOPPED off at the Asparagus Fern Bar & Grill for a nostalgic look at the old swinging singles scene when that famed adventurer Buck Ace strode in, a sense of purpose etched on his chiseled features. I could tell by the resolute set of his cleft chin that he was up to some awesome new feat of derring-do.

"What is it this time, Buck?" I asked. "Scaling the unscalable north face of Mount Parnasse, breasting the fatal waters of the Gowanus Canal, fording the piranha-infested . . ."

He shook his head. "I am bored with humdrum pursuits," he said gravely. "After considerable deliberation I have decided to explore an incredible sexual experience I have never dared attempt before."

"But, Buck," I protested, "what innovations could exist in this field for you, the folk hero of the swinging singles scene, the man who invented group grope, inverse adhesion, and duodynamic suspension?"

"I am surfeited with tiresome repetitiveness," he said with a weary sigh. "I am about to accept the ultimate sexual challenge."

"You don't mean . . ."

"Yes," he said, solemnly downing his Bombay gin and Calcutta water in a single gulp, "marriage."

I couldn't believe my ears. "Buck," I said, "where did you get this crazy idea?"

He slapped the latest issue of *Success Today* on the bar. "Look at this," he said, "a sixteen-page cover story entitled 'Marriage—the Newest Sex Craze.' No respectable magazine would appear on the stands without such an article. *Time* even quotes that great sex researcher Helen Gurley Brown, editor of *Cosmopolitan,* as discovering that 'sex with a commitment is absolutely delicious.'"

"Incredible," I said. "What will these madcap jet-setters dream up next?"

Buck gazed over my shoulder into distant vistas. "The message is clear," he said. "A proposal of marriage is the *ne plus ultra* of turn-ons for a woman. And, as a man, try to imagine overcoming the unbelievable challenges entailed in making love to the same person day after day, night after night."

"It doesn't sound easy," I agreed.

"Neither was crossing the North Atlantic in a hot tub," said Buck airily. "My soul won't rest until I make the supreme effort to enter realms of sensation I have never entered before. And you shall witness the historic first step on this awesome adventure."

"Think first, Buck!" I cried. "Think of us old married men who have idolized you so long."

But to no avail. With the same devil-may-care grin he had flashed as he leapt without a parachute from the bay of a B–24 over burning Dresden, he turned to the attractive young woman on the bar stool next to him and in practiced tones murmured, "By the way you grasp the stem of your frozen banana daiquiri you must have a smashing backhand in racquetball. How would you like to split this tawdry scene and indulge in a little marriage with me?"

The effect was instantaneous. Her eyes moistened; the pulse in her throat quickened; and her lips parted in eager anticipation. "I couldn't be more in the mood," she gasped.

He took her hand in his. "Have you ever tried eternal commitment with total communication?" he whispered. "I will show you its myriad delights. And, believe me, I will always respect you."

"Please be gentle" was all she could say.

It was enough. He gazed deeply into her eyes and breathed those four little words that mean ever so much these days on the swinging singles scene, "Your chapel or mine?"

As I watched the excited couple slip out into the night on their thrillingly hazardous escapade, I raised my glass in a silent toast to the Sexual Revolution. Just think, it took only a couple of decades of the Sexual Revolution to make marriage look good.

And to more and more Americans every day it does look good. From Bangor to Burbank, from Maui to Miami, official records show that people are getting married who have never gotten married before. What lies behind this incredible phenomenon? Responsible sociologists agree that the Sexual Revolution assuredly plays an important role. "Like most successful revolutions, the Sexual Revolution has bred a counter revolution," says Dr. Homer T. Pettibone, dean of cultural psychosociology at Skarewe University. "After years in the front lines of sexual exploration and experimentation, the young revolutionaries of the sixties and seventies have grown more responsible, more mature, and more conscious of their debts to society. Or, to put it in lay terms, they've grown just plain tired."

A case in point is that well-known single swinger, Spurgeon Kinsley. As it must to all men, middle age finally crept up on Spurgeon. "It isn't the accumulation of years I mind so much," he said with a sigh. "It's the accumulation of baggage."

In his salad days, Spurgeon would arrive at the Asparagus Fern Bar & Grill wearing a T-shirt, jeans, and a pair of Adidas without socks—ready and eager for an hour, a night, or a whatever of romance, whenever, wherever, and with whomever.

But gradually, almost imperceptibly, time weighed him down. He found he needed a jacket so he'd have pockets for his nasal spray and dental floss. Then he began carrying a briefcase to hold his back brace, Vitamin E, and Dr. Scholl's assorted podiatric aids.

His adventures, needless to say, were becoming further and further apart. The end came when he finally inveigled Lorelei Beburn, a comely young management trainee, to ask him up to her apartment for "a little nightcap."

"I'd really love to," said Spurgeon enthusiastically in response to her invitation. "Wait till I get my suitcase."

Once in Miss Beburn's apartment, Spurgeon employed his years of experience in such matters to charm her right out of her—in a word—reluctance. "Why don't you just tuck yourself in," said Spurgeon, happily opening his suitcase, "while I plug in my contact lens electric sterilizer? Darn, do you happen to have any Flexi-Care Saline Solution? My bottle seems to be running low. And are there another couple of outlets somewhere for my Water-Pik and blow drier?"

"Are you coming to bed soon?" inquired Miss Beburn with more curiosity than ardor.

"In a minute," said Spurgeon. But as soon as he had his contacts bubbling merrily away, his teeth thoroughly Water-Pik'd, and his bald spot blown dry, he brought forth his box of medications. "Let's see," he said, unscrewing caps, "one blue one, two yellows, this speckled baby and . . . Oh, yes, I'd better have this white nitroglycerin number handy on the nightstand in case you turn out to be a real, ha, ha, bombshell. There we are. Now, I'll just stretch out here . . ."

"Tell me something," murmured Miss Beburn. "Why,

if I'm stretched out in this bed, are you stretched out on that floor?"

"The old lower back," gasped Spurgeon. "Have to do a hundred of these sit-ups at bedtime or the darned thing goes out on me. Ninety-eight ... ninety-nine ... There! Now, just fifty lifts with this five-pound weight for my tennis elbow and I'll be with you, Lorelei honey. Lorelei, honey? Lorelei?"

But Miss Beburn had slipped off to Artie's Break Dancing Palace where she lost three pounds and the rest of her reluctance to a twenty-four-year-old sidewalk artist who was wearing a T-shirt, jeans, and Adidas without socks.

Poor Spurgeon. He became known as the Strike-Out King of the Asparagus Fern. And he retired to a corner behind the espresso machine where he deliberately attempted to take his own sanity with an old Rubik's Cube.

"Turn the green row to the left," a soft, sweet voice murmured in his ear one evening. He looked up into the attractively mature face of Fiona Stovelow.

"My place or my place?" said Spurgeon. "For, like a delicate Beaujolais, I don't seem to travel well anymore."

Once there, Spurgeon apologetically explained that he would need a brief recess in order to sterilize, pick, blow dry, medicate, and exercise himself.

"Oh, please don't hurry," said Miss Stovelow. With that, she opened her voluminous carry-all and arranged on the dresser her cleansing cream, moisturizer, wrinkle remover, frown preventer, Porcelana, hand cream, bifocals, Tums, arthritis pills, duplicate prescriptions, Band-Aids, Kleenex, shower cap, hair net, eye drops, and oceans and oceans of lotions and potions.

"Darling!" cried Spurgeon, taking her in his arms. "We were made for each other!"

So they were married and lived happily ever after—massaging each other's backs, filling each other's hot water bottles, and helping each other pack the U-Haul trailer they rented for intimate little weekends in the country.

There are, of course, numerous other valid reasons for getting married. When I was young, a common one was dot, dot, dot. You know, "He took her into his arms and dot, dot, dot." In those primitive days when sex education was a peer group activity, few of us adolescents were confident of our ability to dot, dot, dot correctly. The ignorance of some young ladies was astounding. I recall particularly the sad tale of Millicent G., who was so carried away on the rosy clouds of love that she allowed Jimmy N. to kiss her goodnight on their first date.

"Good heavens!" cried Millicent when restored to her senses. "Now I'll have a baby!"

"No, you won't," said Jimmy, who was a sly boot. "Not if you take the proper precautions."

"Oh," wailed poor Millicent, "what are they?"

"Never fear, I'll show you," said Jimmy. And he did. But she had a baby anyway.

Another, and, I feel, equally valid reason for getting married is palimony. In the good old male chauvinist pig days, a man simply kept a mistress. He plied her with diamonds, drank champagne out of her slipper if he had a strong stomach, and when she had too much mileage on her, turned her in on a new model. This seemed a clear-cut, fair-minded relationship that was well understood by both parties. For some reason, however, women found it unappealing. (As a frustrated Freud so aptly asked at the end of his long career, "What do women want?") Consequently, the scene at the Asparagus Fern Bar & Grill has changed radically in recent years. One of the first to notice the difference was Herbert Namewithheld, who dropped in the other evening in search of, as was his wont, a Jack Daniels over ice and a companion overnight. His preference for the latter was one Hermione F., a comely figure skater who was into doing Roman numerals.

"I started with II," she confided between sips of her Chablis, "and I quickly discovered I had a talent for it. I feel that once I have conquered X, I'll have it made."

"I cannot live without you," replied Herbert, that being his standard opening line. "Let us have a lasting, meaningful relationship."

"Meaning," interposed the balding gentleman on Herbert's left as he opened a briefcase, "one that could even last over a long weekend."

"Are you his father?" inquired Hermione nervously.

"No, I'm his attorney, Nick Pitnick," said the gentleman, handing her a card. "And if you are interested in his terms, I am prepared to draw up a binding contract."

"What about my budding career?" asked Hermione with a wily look. "Does he wish me to give it up in order to make a better weekend home for him?"

"Oh, darling, would you?" cried the impetuous Herbert.

"He means," said Pitnick, "would you, Hermione, continue your pursuit of the impossible dream until you have conquered MMCMXCVIII and have been rewarded with Social Security and financial independence?"

"Darn," said Hermione.

"Furthermore," said Pitnick, "you must promise never to change your name to his."

"Don't be silly," said Hermione. "Who would hire a beautiful blonde figure skating star name Herbert?"

"Wonderful," said Herbert, downing his drink. "Then we're all set."

"Hold it," said Hermione. "Do you want to have a baby?"

"Not tonight; it would be a headache," said Pitnick, "legally speaking."

"Okay," said Hermione with a shrug, "your place or mine?"

"An interesting question," conceded Pitnick. "Let us compare their net values."

Herbert and Hermione were married a week later. Herbert said he had always enjoyed the romance and daring of meaningful relationships, but recently they had become considerably less romantic and considerably more daring. "And there's one thing you can say for marriage," said Herbert. "It's a hell of a lot simpler."

This is not, let me hasten to add, the only thing you can say in favor of marriage. Another thing you can say in favor of marriage is that it confers clear-cut, concise titles on the participants, i.e., "husband," in the case of men, and "wife," in the case of others. One of the most compelling reasons for getting married today is that there is no adequate term to describe the person you are living with in sin. While living in sin carries no scarlet letter in this enlightened day and age, it definitely carries a heavy burden when it comes to introductions: "Hi, I want you to meet the person with whom I'm living in sin." This simply won't do. And much has been written about the highly offensive inoffensiveness of such substitutes as "friend," "roommate," "beau" or that awful "posslq." Indeed, I knew a young lady who, in desperation, took to referring to the young gentleman with whom she was living in sin as her whatchamacallhim. When Whatchamacallhim (a.k.a., Schuyler) objected, she said, well, they could always get married. Whatchamacallhim said testily that a wedding was only a bunch of mumbo-jumbo words solemnized by a scrap of paper. She said if that's all a wedding was, why not have one so she wouldn't have to introduce him as her whatchamacallhim? He could think of but one logical recourse and that was to yield reluctantly. Thus she now has no problem with her introductions: "Hi," she says, "I want you to meet Schuyler."

Let me say right here that where my children are concerned I'm definitely against their living with others without the benefit of wedlock. There are two reasons for this. I tried to explain the first to our son, Mordred, when he announced that he and a comely young lady named Philomel had, after long deliberation, decided to abandon their "meaningful relationship" in favor of a "committed relationship." It took some questioning to determine this meant they were now committed to sharing their joys, their heartaches, their toothpaste, and their rent until death or some whim did them part.

Instead of saying, "That's nice," the way sophisticated parents are required to do, I took the bull by the horns and said, "Why don't you get married?"

Mordred, of course, looked at me aghast. "I don't believe it!" he cried. "Would you really expect us to pay $28.00 for a lousy scrap of paper signifying the government approves of our lifestyle?"

"Don't think of it as a scrap of paper, Mordred," I said. "Think of it as an investment."

"An investment?" asked Mordred, who is nothing if not mercenary. "An investment in what?"

"Waring blenders," I said.

Mordred and Philomel looked at each other with arched eyebrows. "Waring Blendors?" said Philomel.

"When Mordred's dear mother and I got married," I explained, "assorted friends and relatives gave us no fewer than nine blenders—six Harvest Gold and three Avocado Green. Seeing that times are better, you and Philomel should net a dozen."

"What are we going to do with a dozen blenders?" asked Philomel.

"Why, give them away, of course," I said.

"What's in the fridge?" asked Mordred, heading for the kitchen.

"Not all at once," I added hastily. "You give them away over the years to your friends who are getting married."

That stopped him. "My friends?" he said. "Getting married?"

"You never know, Mordred," I said. "For there is an inexplicable rule in life that, no matter how big your wedding, you never get as many wedding presents as you will eventually be forced to give to your friends, your friends' children, and, if you live long enough, your friends' children's children. And don't forget what loot Philomel will drag in from kitchen showers."

I could tell he was getting interested. "Maybe we could send out engraved announcements of our committed relationship," he said hopefully, "along with little At Home cards so people will know where to send gifts."

"Nobody gives you anything for living in sin, Mordred," I said sternly, "except advice."

"I hate weddings," he said. "Flat champagne, soggy cake . . ."

"Everybody hates weddings," I said. "The only reason to have one is so that on your death bed you can smile with satisfaction—the satisfaction of knowing that you almost came out even."

"And that's the best I can hope for?" asked Mordred.

"Play your cards right, kid," I said, "and your mother and I will throw in a Cuisinart."

Needless to say, that was not the major reason I wished my children to get married rather than live in sin. The major one is agonizingly familiar to any parent in similar straits these days. Our daughter, Malphasia, for example, could hardly wait to reach the age of consent so that she could consent to run off to New York, where she took up housekeeping with a struggling young author named Beowulf, who was struggling to learn how to spell. Malphasia changed her name to "Ms.," took a position as a window dresser at McDonald's, and settled down to the enjoyment of sin. We wrote her regularly and cheerily to show how broadminded we were. And although we had to address her letters to her in care of Beowulf as the apartment was in his name, no mention of him ever wormed its way inside the envelope. When friends asked how Malphasia was, we'd report she was living in New York.

"The poor thing, all alone in that big city?" a well-intentioned lady might ask.

"Oh, no, she has a roommate."

"And what's her name?"

"Malphasia."

"No, I meant her roommate."

"I think it starts with a B."

Then came the fateful letter. Malphasia and Beowulf were coming to visit. My dear wife, Glynda, asked the question that has rocked thousands upon thousands of American households these past several decades:

"Where will they sleep?"

When Malphasia and Beowulf arrived one evening, they found both of us at the door nervously beaming. "Now you just take your suitcase right up to your room, dear," said Glynda. "We've kept it just the way you left it, with your tiny, narrow, little, single bed and all."

"But I had twin beds, Mother," protested Malphasia.

"Oh, we moved the other downstairs to change the decor," I explained. "Don't you think it looks nice?"

"In the middle of the living room?" asked Malphasia.

"And there's your towel, Beowulf, on the coffee table," said Glynda. "Just put your bag on the sofa."

"My, it's eight o'clock already," I said, yawning hastily, "I think I'll hit the old sack."

It was a very long night. "Did you hear something?" I inquired about 11:00 P.M.

"Maybe it's a burglar?" suggested Glynda.

"I hope so," I said. And several hours later I added that I thought I smelled smoke.

"I think it's best to ignore it," said Glynda.

"I wish I could go get a glass of water," I said.

We were awake at dawn, but thought we'd loll about in bed until nine in order to be sure the others were up and in their proper places. We were so bleary from lack of sleep when we finally came downstairs that we had difficulty understanding Malphasia when she finally broke the news:

"We came home to tell you that Beowulf and I are talking about getting married," she said. "What would you think about us having a big, formal wedding?"

Glynda said that would cost several thousand dollars. But you know how daddies are. "If that's what you want, dear, you go right ahead," I said in a fatherly fashion. "We just want to make you happy."

I told a somewhat surprised Glynda later that I felt it would be money well spent. "After all, we're not losing a daughter," I said happily. "We're gaining a good night's sleep."

So much for the major reasons for getting married. To be fair, I should cite at least one reason for not getting married. That reason is divorce. All reputable studies indicate that the major cause of divorce is marriage. It is perhaps for this seemingly valid reason that so many couples live together these days without getting married. I feel strongly that they are making a mistake. For when you get right down to it, it's not getting married that triggers the suit for divorce, it's living together. Thus many happily married couples are solving that problem today by not living together *after* marriage. "With both of us working together in the kitchen, we used to get into constant fights over how much MSG to put in the Imperial Dragon-Phoenix Chicken of the Seven Treasures," says Jenny Ng of Canton, Ohio, whose husband, Harry, now lives in Canton, China. "But not anymore." Asked if she believed in young couples living together before marriage, Mrs. Ng shrugged. "What's the difference?" she said.

So in these confusing times, it is comforting to know that there are still a few traditionalists around who cling to the old-fashioned reasons for getting married, reasons that have been tested by mankind down through the generations. When I think of these upholders of the ancient verities, I think of my old pal, Milton Haberdash, although, to tell the truth, you could have knocked me over with a feather when I heard he was getting married. Milt's the guy who runs the football pool, loans you *Playboy,* and provides the cabin for the stag weekends of our Universal Peace Through Oneness & Separate Checks Dining Club. We all thought of Milt as the whiskey-drinking, cigar-smoking, perennial bachelor.

"Congratulations, Milt," I said, clapping him on the shoulder when I ran into him in the office elevator. "I always said that some day you'd discover you need a soulmate with whom to share life's triumphs and tribulations."

"I need a wife," said Milt.

"Exactly," I said. "And who's the lovely little lady?"

"I haven't found one yet," he said.

"I'm sure you will," I said. "But what brought on this monumental decision? A desire for children? A fear of loneliness? A realization that two against the world is better than one?"

Milt scowled thoughtfully. "Actually," he said, "I was sitting home reading *Inside Bowling* and the only 100-watt globe in the place went out."

"And you felt the need then and there for someone to cuddle up with in the darkness!" I cried triumphantly.

"No," said Milt, "I felt the need then and there for someone to remember to buy 100-watt light bulbs."

I was slightly taken aback. "A wife, Milt," I said sternly, "does more for a man than remember to buy 100-watt light bulbs."

"I certainly hope so," he said. "I also need someone to get my prescriptions filled, take the car in, call my mother once a week, and be home between 8:00 and 12:00 and 1:00 and 4:00 when the dishwasher breaks down."

"Why don't you just hire a personal servant?" I inquired with a touch of sarcasm.

"On my salary I couldn't afford the minimum wage for a forty-hour week, much less overtime."

"Overtime?"

"I figure it would also be handy to have someone who'd cater parties for the people I owe dinners, clean my closets,

buy wedding presents for my cousins, and pick the burrs
off the dog."

I was shocked. "Milt," I said, "you're twenty years behind the times. We liberated men have long since re-
nounced oppressing members of the opposite sex."

Milt looked at me. "Why?" he asked.

"Because," I explained. He was still looking at me.
"Let's see," I said. "Because oppressing women burdened
us with hidden guilt feelings."

"I'd much rather be burdened with a few hidden guilt
feelings than write one more thank-you note to my Aunt
Miranda-Jane for three lousy handkerchiefs every
Christmas," said Milt. "Anyway, who decided we
shouldn't oppress women?"

I shrugged. "Women, I guess. They wanted to free us
from the narrow stereotyped role of the powerful father
figure who makes all the decisions."

Milt nodded. "Darned decent of them," he said. "But
one thing puzzles me about this business of oppressed
people always asking their oppressors to knock off oppressing them."

"There's nothing puzzling about that, Milt," I said.
"Where else would they turn?"

"Oh, that's not what puzzles me," said Milt. "What
puzzles me is why oppressors ever give up the good thing
they've got going."

Well, Milton Haberdash is obviously a no-good, rotten,
male chauvinist pig, a man who should be held up to the
universal opprobrium of all fair-minded people. And he
will certainly never find the girl of his dreams, not in this

liberated day and age. But his arguments did strike me as mildly intriguing. So I went home and asked my dear wife, Glynda, if she'd mind if I oppressed her a bit now and then.

Glynda thoughtfully speared the olive in her martini with a toothpick. "Go give yourself a backrub," she said.

CHAPTER TWO

Choosing the Right Spouse for You

SO YOU'VE READ Chapter One and you've decided to get married. Good for you. The next step is more difficult: You must now choose *whom* to marry. I don't wish to make you nervous, but this is a very, very important decision. As a matter of fact, the rest of your life depends upon it. *And it isn't as easy as it sounds.* The uninitiated might think they could simply wander into a butcher shop, say, espy an attractive person of the opposite sex purchasing chicken livers, and bring off some riposte like: "Hey! You want to get married?" But it doesn't work like this and that's a shame. For, contrary to all logic, millions and millions of people persist every year in getting married for the worst of all possible reasons: love.

Let me say immediately before I'm accused of being an old grump that I have nothing against romantic love *per se*. Romantic love has produced more art, more theater, and more literature than any other aspect of the human condition. Besides, it's lots of fun. Pursuing or being pursued through the maze of courtship has Hares and Hounds or even Scrabble beat all hollow. And I sincerely hope that every young person has the opportunity to undergo this experience. Once. On the other hand, it should be mentioned that for millennia romantic love has been the sole cause of all crimes of passion, as well as countless suicides, innumerable divorces, and the Trojan War. Down through the centuries, it has proved to be the most monumental waste of time, energy, and money in human history. If mankind had devoted half the effort it spent on romantic love to worthwhile causes, it would have long since eliminated poverty, disease, most bad poetry, and the feminine headache.

But, as I say, I have nothing against romantic love. All I ask is that you, in choosing a spouse, keep in mind that anyone in love suffers from severe impairment of his or her decision-making process. Or, to put it in psychiatric terms, they're cuckoo. The primary symptom of romantic love is manic-depression, which is, of course, a condition associated with severe mental illness. Observe the person in love: He or she is either irrationally happy when things are going well or irrationally unhappy when they are not. The significant fact here is that the person in love is, *ipso facto,* irrational and thus incapable of making any but irrational decisions.

Now there are undoubtedly some misogamists out there who will say, "Well, that's the only conceivable state of mind to be in for any danged idiot fool enough to consider getting married." Not I. What I say is that romantic love is, at best, a transitory emotion. The more intensely it flames in the heart, the faster it burns itself out. Thus those who marry in the heat of romantic love are doomed to spend their wedded life poking through its clammy ashes.

This, in turn, engenders only bitterness. Any used car buyer knows the progression: There is that first cautious approach, followed by the stirrings of desire. Perhaps this is the right car for you? You touch; you stroke; you take it for a trial spin. Yes! Yes, this is the only car in the world, the one you want to spend the rest of your life with. You blindly take the plunge in a simple little ceremony. You drive from the lot in this best of all possible cars, your soul filled with music as the tires whisper on the pavement and the steady, trustworthy engine hums its love song. Then the muffler falls off. Well, no car's perfect. It's still a darned good car. Maybe not a great car, but a good car and you're lucky. . . . You're lucky there's a phone only six miles down the road when the fan belt breaks at 2:00 A.M. in the middle of the great Mojave Desert. And by the time the transmission goes, which it invariably does, you feel betrayed. Your wisdom has been proven impaired, your judgment faulty. Can you conceivably go on loving the evidence of your own credulity? It's fortunate you don't take an axe to it. Of course, you may go on reluctantly living with it, but only because you have gradually become adjusted to its being, at the very best, just another car. Indeed, the only thing that saves the institution of marriage and the used car business is that the defects in the loved object reveal themselves one at a time.

Lord knows, I tried to put all this across to our son, Mordred, the evening he came home with the announcement that he and Philomel had at last decided to get married. It was a Thursday and Glynda was at her real estate class. So I was on my own.

"That's wonderful, Mordred," I said, shaking his hand. "What color Cuisinart would you like?"

"A pox on material possessions, Dad," said Mordred grandly, as he exchanged a look of adoration with Philomel. "We plan to get married because we are madly, passionately in love."

"Good grief, Mordred," I said. "That's the best reason in the world *not* to get married. Nothing clouds the old brain more than mad, passionate love. And here you are deciding whom to spend the rest of your life with when you can't think straight."

"Our all-consuming love will fuse us in oneness," said Philomel with the positiveness of youth.

"For about three weeks," I agreed. "And once this all-consuming love consumes all, including itself, you will look on each other with suspicion, distrust, and possibly downright loathing. When you begin life together with a handicap like that, you'll never be able to tolerate him flossing his teeth in the living room."

"He flosses in the living room?" she asked, her eyes widening.

"I don't know," I said. "But the point is you must be able to tolerate it—just as Mordred must be willing to pop your back after a hard day at the office."

"My back doesn't need popping," she said with a touch of asperity.

"Not yet," I said. "And Mordred doesn't yet need glasses. But when he does, will you rummage about, three or four times a day, trying to figure out where he left them?"

"Can't he find his own glasses all by himself?" demanded Philomel.

"Certainly," I said. "But then why get married?"

I suspected they didn't know what I was talking about. I was right. "Look, Dad," said Mordred, "We're going to promise to love, honor, and cherish each other until death do us part."

"That's nice," I said. "Will you also promise to walk her dog in the rain when she's had her hair done? And how about surprising her by tying up the papers when it's her turn? Or mincing up the garlic and honey when she's got a sore throat?"

"Do you really think that's all marriage is about?" asked Mordred with a touch of disbelief.

"No, not all," I said. "It also includes locking the clasp on her bracelet every time you go out. She could do it with one hand, but you can do it more easily with two. That's why you also willingly hook her dress at the back of her neck and pull off her rainboots."

"I was planning on being her husband, not her batman," said Mordred, his machismo showing.

"What's the difference?" I said. "Moreover, it isn't simply what you do for each other, but how you do it. For example, Mordred, do you think you could explain 'antidisestablishmentarianism' to her without sounding patronizing?"

"Couldn't I just bring her breakfast in bed?" said Mordred sulkily.

"Breakfast in bed is highly overrated," I told him. "Far more challenging is to arise at 2:00 A.M. to give the baby its bottle without moaning in agony so that she awakens to learn of your suffering."

It was clever Philomel who at last caught a glimmer of my deep philosophical message. "Okay," she said with a little sigh as she removed her hand from Mordred's. "We'll both floss in the living room."

When Glynda came home, I recounted the whole sad conversation. "Don't worry," she said with her indomitable optimism as she stashed away her binder, "I'm sure it will work out all right."

"Maybe," I said. "But I seriously doubt a marriage can long endure that is based solely on flossing together in the living room."

She gave me half a smile and a peck on the cheek. "You forget," she said, "we didn't even have that."

I suppose we didn't. In those long-gone days, we kissed on the second date, necked on the tenth, and, in a moment of blind, undying passion, became engaged on the twentieth. There followed several months of sheer hell toward the end of which the happy couple had usually developed a deep aversion, if not yet an abiding loathing, for each

other. But the announcements had been made, the showers had been held, the cake had been baked, and the two
sets of parents were sitting in their pews with expectant
expressions. I remember thinking as I stood before the
altar that marriage was the supreme test of courage. And
those who failed it got married.

Even back then, though, we talked of Margaret Mead's
daring proposal for trial marriage. That is, we young gen-
tlemen talked about it. We wouldn't dream of talking
about it with our young ladies, particularly, God forbid,
our fiancées. After all, sexual acts were lewd, lascivious,
and obscene. And how could we share with a young lady
the prospect of committing lewd, lascivious, and obscene
acts upon her eternally lovable, honorable, and cherish-
able body?

So we blithely got married without knowing whether
our life partner was, to put it bluntly, good in bed. Today,
of course, entire books are being written on the subject.
One recent one, of which I haven't heard much lately is
What Makes a Woman Good in Bed by the British author
Wendy Leigh. In her introduction, Ms. Leigh says she
bases her findings on "face-to-face interviews" with more
than a hundred of "the world's top celebrities," who pre-
sumably know as much about the subject as anyone. I
may be prejudiced but I feel this attribute of a prospective
spouse is of limited interest. For Ms. Leigh, like her fellow
experts in the field, confines her inquiry on what makes a
woman good in bed to those moments when the woman
and her partner are both awake. This condition, after all,
applies to only the briefest of interludes in the marital

27 ———

day. Indeed, I am able to base my conclusions on the topic on a single face-to-face interview with my Aunt Cora, one of the world's top aunts.

"You slept around a lot in your day, Aunt Cora," I said for openers, "you having accompanied your late husband, Bert, on his rounds as a traveling salesman. Tell me, were you good in bed?"

"You bet your buttonhooks, Buster," said Aunt Cora, who does not believe in hiding her light under a bushel. "Not once in fifty-one years did I snore, turn over vigorously, jerk the covers my way, eat, drink, smoke, read, complain about the temperature, hear strange sounds, or smell something funny after retiring. These modern young flibbertigibbets could learn a lot from my generation."

You bet they could! And I think that adequately takes care of what makes a woman good in bed. Of far more importance, I believe, is what makes a woman good in bathroom. I will pass over the standard criteria—such as does she put the curtain inside the tub when showering or does she clutter up the sink with tubes and vials and boxes and jars—in order to get to the heart of the matter: that cylinder of what advertisers genteelly term "bathroom tissue." Here's where a good woman is hard to find.

Call me a sexist if you will, but after conducting face-to-face interviews with more than one hundred of the world's top husbands, I've concluded that women, upon using the last tissue on a roll, tend to go airily on their way without so much as a thought to those who will come after. This is not only selfish, it's downright cheating. After a few shouting matches, they may condescend to leave a fresh roll (still in its package) on the floor beneath the holder. If you do somehow finally manage to cow them into installing the new roll where it belongs, they invariably install it upside-down with the tissue emerging from the bottom. You then have to take the entire mechanism apart and undergo a roll reversal, which invariably entails a severe trauma.

Eventually, after years of threats and supplication, you may some day be rewarded by finding a fresh roll in its proper place *right-side up!* If you do, you will also find that the spindle has not been adequately secured in the holder and when you tug on the tissue, the whole contraption flies off the wall, scattering parts all over the bathroom floor. Indeed, it is my contention that bathroom tissue is the prime cause for divorce in America today. And if not divorce, then murder.

In addition to what makes a woman good in bathroom, you should also consider when seeking a spouse what makes a woman good in kitchen. Here we find that the ideal woman lets herself be swept away not only by her passion for gourmet cooking on an infinitesimal budget but also washing, drying, and picking every last shred of broccoli out of the sink strainer. Chores should be shared, however, and she should always ask the man to unscrew the lid on the pickle jar (but only after she has secretly loosened it first). Other questions to keep in mind are what makes a woman good in garden (a love of honest toil is helpful here) and what makes a woman good in breakfast nook (silence and a fascination with the Modern Living section of the morning paper). And I must say that my dear wife, Glynda, is particularly good in living room. Many is the Monday night that I've come home to find her intently watching professional football on the television screen, her book ignored in her lap, her absorption total.

"Who's ahead?" I'll ask her.

"I don't know," she'll say. "Who's playing?"

So, frankly, I don't understand this preoccupation our society has with beds. Beds are certainly a part of our daily lives, but only a small part. I don't care how good a woman is in bed if she can't meet my criteria for what makes a woman good in Italian restaurant. In this respect, if she eats ravioli with her fingers, I say the hell with her.

Lord knows, I tried to impart to my children the necessity of picking a spouse with all the cool reason they could muster. "If you must determine whether or not you and some young man are compatible," I told Malphasia, "don't run off for a weekend at some romantic resort; go camping in the rain." My efforts, however, were to little avail. I don't blame my theory; I blame my children. Take the time Malphasia had a blind date. The whole family was nervous, as she was getting into the marrying years. Being a good father, I naturally sat her down for an open, earnest, useless, heart-to-heart talk:

"Malphasia," I said, "it is high time you assessed your goals in life and logically decided precisely what sort of man would best help you attain them."

"Oh, but I have, Daddy," she said. "The man I marry must have piercing blue eyes like Paul Newman, soft curly hair like Tom Selleck and a devil-may-care grin like Harrison Ford."

"That's just fine, dear," I said. "But seeing that he will be the father of your children, don't you think you might also give some thought to his character?"

"Sure, Daddy," she said. "He'll also have to be tender and romantic. I know I could never relate to anyone who didn't love dancing cheek-to-cheek, gerbils, Woody Allen movies, and Snake Pitt & the Expectorators."

"I'm sure Snake Pitt & the Expectorators have their place in any mature relationship," I said. "But reason dictates that if you must marry for love, you should love someone with good prospects. You really should choose a young man in an expanding field who will go far."

At this, Malphasia clapped her hands. "How did you know, Daddy?" she cried. "I've always secretly wanted to meet a professional balloon racer who would take me soaring far above this humdrum world to exotic, sun-kissed lands."

"That sounds like an exciting job," I agreed, "if not very steady. What would you say to a fellow in the military parts supply business who, if he made one sale of a dozen gearshift knobs for the M–1 tank, could retire for life?"

"I'd say, 'Don't call me; I'll call you,' " said Malphasia. "Really, Daddy, who cares about making money in some dull old job?"

"Making money, dear girl," I said, "beats making beds, making Tuna Surprise, and making do in some wretched little flat above a store."

"Poof," she said with the disdain for reality of starry-eyed youth. "The man for me must be tall, handsome, tender, romantic, and love all the things in life that I love. What else matters?"

Like any good father, I couldn't help worrying that the evening's blind date would turn out to be the man of her dreams, and we would lose her to this shallow substitute for a decent, respectable, good provider.

Poor Malphasia. When her blind date arrived, I had a few words with him while she was upstairs applying the finishing touches. His name was Petrid Fentris and the only thing he and Malphasia had in common, as far as I could tell, was that he faintly resembled Woody Allen— the same thick glasses, the same wispy hair, and the same dirty tennis shoes. He turned out to be pigeon census taker for the Parks Department. In his favor, he loathed Snake Pitt & the Expectorators and looked upon gerbils as immature rats. His favorite avocation was break dancing to "The Collected Works of Mantovani" and the farthest he had been off the ground was a four-foot stepladder as his fear of heights bordered on paranoia. Here, certainly, was the last young man on earth for Malphasia.

"There is a God in heaven looking over us," I said with a contented sigh to Glynda after Malphasia and Petrid had gone out the door.

As for Petrid, Malphasia, of course, adored him.

So you can see the problem: Young people are simply too immature to select the proper criteria for picking a spouse and far too flighty to stick to the improper criteria they have selected. Or, to put it another way, they're hopeless. A far more reasonable alternative would be to have the task of spouse-picking turned over to much wiser, more experienced, concerned-but-unbiased judges of human nature. Namely, parents. Since the dawn of history, parents have traditionally performed this chore. And, while it has not worked out in every single case (see Henry VIII and Catharine of Aragon), certainly graying adults in their forties or fifties are better qualified in this all-important field than love-blinded snippets not yet dry behind the ears (see Romeo and Juliet). In the past hundred years, unfortunately, the little-heralded generational revolution has all but put an end to this exemplary practice. Children have become downright uppity. In my own case, I have been tempted on occasion to suggest to Mordred that we go down to the Asparagus Fern Bar & Grill and check over the prospective spouse supply together on his behalf. But seeing with what vigor he has declined his mother's generous offer to help him pick out a jacket, a pair of trousers, or a haircut, I have gamely resisted the urge. Until the younger generation comes to its senses—and I am not holding my breath—parental guidance will be limited to suggesting movies children shouldn't attend but undoubtedly will. Yet, there is hope. There is hope that we parents may be replaced by that new universal friend of mankind, the computer.

A pioneer in this field is my young friend, Auger. Growing up in a computerized world, Auger was computer literate at an early age and even computer friendly. So while he had the skepticism of parental wisdom that seems universal among our youth, he also had a blind faith in the interaction of silicon chips. On reaching puberty, he made several efforts to pick out the woman of his dreams by the old process of random selection. None was successful. When he saw an advertisement in *Swingles* magazine for "Comput-a-Date," he immediately saw the error of his ways. He then. . . . But let Auger tell his story in his own words:

When I spotted that ad (he begins), I instinctively knew that the major challenge of my life would now be resolved. All my worries were over, my cares in the hands—or, more accurately, the circuitry—of a benign and infallible spirit. I suppose I felt a little like a man entering a monastery. So I dialed an 800 number and spoke to an answering machine. Three days later, a computerized bundle addressed to "Dear Friend" arrived in the mail. It took me a good three hours to fill in the sixty-four pages of information the computer requested. You can't imagine the intimate details involved in the questions: "How many times a day did I brush my teeth? Once? Twice? Three times? Rarely?" It was comforting to know that I would be dealing with an omniscient data processor.

I mailed the information back special delivery. The next two nights I hardly slept. Then a Mr. Knockman from Comput-a-Date called. It was a bit disconcerting speaking to a human being, but the news he bore was overwhelmingly reassuring:

"We've had couples in the ninety-eighth percentile," he said, "but we've never before hit a hundred. I wish you could have seen the big board light up and flash over and over again: 'PERFECT INTERFACE . . . PERFECT INTERFACE. . . .' "

Knockman told me that the name of this paragon of admirable traits was Roxanne Baumeister. "Like you," he said, "she's a twenty-three-year-old, intelligent, moderate Republican who wants three children (two boys and a girl), and loves walking in the rain, Cheez-Its, and watching Japanese monster movies on late-night television."

"How many times a day does she brush her teeth?" I asked.

"Mornings and evenings," he said.

"Incredible!"

Needless to say, I couldn't wait to see what the woman of my dreams looked like. I called to ask her if she'd like to attend the local Geological Society's Rock Festival, which I knew that I, and therefore she, would like to attend. Her voice had that soft, throaty quality that I love. "Of course," was all she said.

When she opened the door, I was stunned. She had precisely the kind of straight blonde hair and Roman nose that I adore. Her dress and perfume were exquisite, her demeanor all that I could desire. I almost took her into my arms then and there and she later told me she was surprised when I didn't. Three dates later I popped the question.

"Roxanne," I said, "we are so ideally suited in all the areas of an interpersonal relationship that I feel we should spend the rest of our lives together getting to know the little things about each other."

She smiled. "Of course," she said.

Well, the first little thing I learned about her was that she dumped the knives, forks, and spoons into the silverware drawer all higgledy-piggledly. "Look, darling," I said as I shook the jumbled implements out on the counter and began placing them back one by one, "each group has its own little section of the basket in which it lives, knives here, forks there, spoons over here, all pointing the same way."

"I can't look now, dearest," she said, "as I am too busy trying to scrape the fried egg off your plate which you soaked in hot water instead of cold."

We being newlyweds, such little flaws were not enough to provoke a spat. And I must say that neither of us left the cap off the toothpaste. Unfortunately, Roxanne was given to leaving the caps off felt-tipped pens instead so that whenever I picked up one to jot down an important number, all I got was a dry scratching. When I mentioned this in passing, she accused me of never screwing the lids back on jars after returning them to the refrigerator so that when she picked up one by the lid, all she usually got was the lid, although once she did get a mound of shattered glass and papaya jam on the kitchen floor.

"And you also put half your hangers backward in the closet, dear," she added. "I simply can't stand seeing your jackets facing each other every which way."

"Don't look," I said, a trifle tartly. "And would you mind not tying my socks together? They're supposed to be stuffed one inside the other in a nice, neat ball."

I don't know where Roxanne got this penchant for tying things, but it extended to the plastic bags of leftovers which she knotted at the top. "Getting them open is ruining my teeth," I told her. "And while we're on the subject, buying unwaxed dental floss is an unwise way to save money."

She thought that over and countered with what she obviously felt was a telling argument, "You put too much dirt in the philodendron pot; there's no room for the water. And who, may I ask, threw out *The Botanical Gardens Quarterly?* I wanted their recipe for stewed miner's lettuce."

Perhaps these little spats wouldn't have amounted to much if we enjoyed sleeping together. We didn't. That is, we didn't sleep together. Not after the night I got up and snapped off the air conditioner. That roused her.

"You know I can't sleep with it off," she complained.

"And you know I can't sleep with it on," I coolly informed her, my voice perhaps rising a little.

Her very last words to me were: "On your way out, please close the closet door. I can't stand the thought of all those poor, confused jackets staring at each other."

Well, poor Auger. Today, he hangs around The Bodde Shoppe Health Club, asking young women if they'd mind letting him have peek into their silverware drawers. As for Roxanne, she married a liberal Democrat she met on a blind date. He hates rain and monster movies. All he wants are five girls and a cocker spaniel. Indeed, they have nothing in common but their mutual devotion to air conditioners. Friends say they have never seen a happier couple.

Again, I don't blame my theory. I blame computers. They may be able at any given moment to pinpoint the precise location and predict the future interaction of more than fifteen thousand satellites and chunks of man-made space debris now whirling around our planet in wildly erratic orbits, but the state of the art has a long way to go before they will be able to grasp the complexities of a marital relationship. So if you can't wait, go ahead and take a gamble, which is what marriage has always been. All I say is that if you'd care to improve your odds, open a telephone book, pick up a pin, and have a stab at it.

CHAPTER THREE

Is There Sex After Marriage?

I CANNOT TELL you how often some young person has come up to me with the fascinating question, "Is there sex after marriage, sir?" My answer, designed to reassure them, is "More than enough." But that's only a half truth. That is to say, there is more than enough sex for half the married people in America and, I fear, not nearly enough for the other half. It is this interesting dichotomy that adds spice to all good marriages. That and the urge to kill.

I tumbled on the latter phenomenon when Glynda looked up from the paper one morning at breakfast. "Did you know that the typical marriage that splits up these days lasts an average of seven years?" she asked.

"Of course," I said. "You've heard of the Seven-Year Itch."

"You mean that after seven years one partner or the other wants a new partner?"

"Not so much that," I said. "The trouble is that after the first seven years, the highlights of marriage have been exhausted: the engagement, the showers, the bachelor party, the wedding, the honeymoon, furnishing the nest, producing the little ones. . . . So when the young couple looks down the road all they can see is the dreary prospect of a lifetime of sameness. That's when the weak and the flighty take the easy way out: divorce. But we who are made of sterner stuff grimly stick with it, dutifully abiding by our contractual obligations until death do us part."

"You make it sound so attractive," she said.

"Come, come," I said, reaching across the table to pat her hand, "have you ever thought of divorcing me?"

She shook her head and I could see the light of truth gleam in her eyes. "No," she said firmly. "Murder many times; divorce never."

How true. My studies in this field overwhelmingly indicate that with the exception of but a few kinky marriages, those that endure down through the years are based on love, devotion, and a mutual interest in justifiable homicide. What is wrong, I say, with spilling a dollop of clam chowder on the yellow couch? What is wrong, I find out, is that it's *Manhattan* clam chowder, for God's sake! Ah, dear, sweet Glynda. If looks could kill. (If looks could kill, I am convinced, we would live in a nation of widows and widowers.) For, yes, under the soft, feminine exterior of any decent, self-respecting wife beats the heart of an axe murderess. Behind the gentle eyes of any patient, tolerant husband throbs the wily criminal mind of a Jack the Ripper. Yet few of us old married hands fear we will become the victims of this ultimate dissolution. I think we instinctively realize that the secret of a lasting marriage is neither tolerance, patience, or undying devotion; it is cowardice.

Take our friends, the Stahlquists, a matched pair of modern, civilized cowards. Like any loving couple, they often entertained thoughts of murder, but what, they asked themselves, would society say if they were to carry out their fondest dreams? Then Argus Stahlquist took an est course and became a new man. Gone was the old lethargic Argus who used to sprawl on the couch on a weekend, drinking beer and watching the sport of the season on television. The new, energetic Argus was a demon around the house. In fact, he went so far as to buy a shovel and announce he was going to dig his own swimming pool. That's when Helena left him.

"Don't you care for swimming pools?" I asked her.

"In the garage?" she said.

But for the most part, we old married couples live out our lives in noisy desperation. In contemplating this thought the other evening, I said to Glynda, "Isn't it a sad commentary on the human race to realize that all the loving couples we know would willfully murder each other?"

"No," she said, "I think it's wonderful they don't."

Darn Glynda. When she one-ups me like that, I could kill her.

But back to the less interesting subject of sex, which, of course, has nothing to do with murder unless you are a practicing psychoanalyst. There is much that can be said about sex. First of all, there are two of them. This was never quite realized until the discovery of sex circa 18,044 B.C. by a Cro-Magnon man named Rok in what is now the Club Méditerranée on Corfu. Prior to that date, the human race was kept going solely by lust. And when it came to advancing the cause of evolution, lust worked admirably. The strongest and cleverest male in any tribal unit would rationally select as his mate the female most physically fit for the ardors of childbearing and cavekeeping. Upon feeling inner stirrings, he would rap her firmly on the head to attract her attention, drag her off to his digs, and proceed, with no fuss or nonsense, to propagate the species. Thus, for eons, the strongest, cleverest, most physically fit specimens continued the seemingly inexorable progress of the human race from its simian ancestors.

Then did romantic love raise its ugly head. No longer could women be viewed as mere lust objects and sources of cheap labor. Henceforth, they had to be wooed, won, and cherished. And while this was a great stride forward for those of the feminine persuasion, it was a catastrophe for mankind. For when an amorous swain murmured, "You have eyes like limpid wells of purple passion," he was rarely thinking about the improvement of the breed. How far better for all of us if he, like his forefathers, had continued to seek out a young maiden with twenty-twenty vision instead—not to mention sound teeth, strong bones, and an I.Q. over one hundred.

But say what you will for lust, it is basically dull. And that's why the human race owes so much in this respect to

Rok's club elbow. Upon feeling those inner stirrings on that historic day, Rok automatically reached for his club. But so painful was the tendonitis that racked his elbow (he had been employing the wrong grip on his backhand) that he was unable to lift it. What to do? "Hi," a desperate Rok said to the nearest cavewoman. "Your cave or mine?" In return, she smiled demurely. And thus was sex born.

From the start, sex proved popular. Men—and women even more so—preferred the thrill of the hunt to a bop on the head and the two sexes coexisted swimmingly for ten thousand years. But when Rok CCXCVIII asked a young woman on a spring evening circa 8044 B.C., "Your cave or mine?" he was not particularly concerned when she yawningly replied that she'd just had her hair done. The fact of the matter was that after sex being viewed as a perfectly normal, healthy activity for ten thousand years, it had no more appeal than any other perfectly normal, healthy activity. What saved sex was the invention the following week—perhaps by coincidence, perhaps not—of civilization. For with civilization came the first crude writing. And one of the crudest was Dr. Jay Prurius's book, *Sex Is Dirty*. By convincing the public that sex was dirty—no difficult task—Dr. Prurius was able to make a comfortable fortune selling dirty books.

For the next ten thousand years sex remained dirty and treasured. Men and women devoted most of their waking time from puberty to senility to pursuing a subject that they wouldn't dream of discussing in public. The human race grew and thrived, owing its astonishing success to its indefatigable prurient interest. And then—heaven help us all!—came the Sexual Revolution.

It was these misguided Sexual Revolutionaries who insisted on talking about sex at dinner parties. It was these crazies who announced that sex was no longer dirty, thereby removing all the prurient interest from it. And, for God's sake, what other kind is there? Is it any wonder that the human race, having lost its prurient interest in sex, is now devoting itself to jogging, "Monday Night Football," and other forms of celibacy? Say what you will about sex—and everybody does these days—there simply isn't enough of it going around to justify all the talk about it that's going around.

Now there are a number of Americans, all of them joggers, who will contend that jogging is not a substitute for sex. They are wrong. I merely cite the report of Drs. Albert Johnson and Natalie Majors in *The American Journal of Genitokinetics,* probably the most widely respected publication in its field. The two researchers began with a Gallup Poll indicating that the number of joggers had doubled since 1961. At the same time, the birth rate had decreased alarmingly. Were the two factors interrelated? After interviews in depth with a scientifically chosen sampling of 1,472 joggers, their answer was a resounding yes.

The first phenomenon the two scientists discovered was that the divorce rate among joggers who took up the activity after age thirty-five was more than 2.4 times the norm. In most cases, they said, this was due to the fact that only one spouse, generally the male, engaged in the pursuit. Usually, he would begin with a modest twenty minutes before breakfast and no harm done. But as his wind improved he would extend his jogs to three or four hours, forcing himself to get up at 4:00 A.M., which, in turn, would necessitate his retiring exhausted by eight o'clock the preceding evening. This definitely interfered with marital relations or, as one wife put it, "Boy, did I ever get sick and tired of him saying, 'Not tonight, my feet hurt.' "

Not only does jogging preclude sex, the authors found, but it sublimates it. "Male joggers in particular," they reported, "obviously equate jogging with sex—bragging about their performance with true male chauvinism. How often do we hear the jogger, flushed with pride and perspiration, say something like, " 'Hey, I did three whole laps around the lake! Had to hang in there for more than an hour nonstop. And then, after only a couple of minutes rest, I did it again. Not bad for a guy my age, eh?'

"While joggers will perform the act of jogging alone— and no one who has studied the expression on the face of a solitary jogger will doubt for a moment that a peculiar form of onanism is being practiced here—most prefer to engage in this activity with a partner, or in the case of young 'swingers,' with a group of partners in a veritable orgy of jogging. Oddly enough, the majority prefer jogging with members of their own sex. They see nothing 'queer' about this, however, and it is certainly not within our purview to comment on the sexual preferences of joggers. *Chacun a son gout,* we say."

On the other hand, if jogging were not an adequate substitute for sex, so many Americans would not be doing

45 ————

it. After all, it is just as sweaty, just as exhausting, just as hard on a lady's coiffure, and just as silly looking. It has, therefore, much to recommend it.

What does worry me is the two researchers' contention that jogging enlarges the heart, striates the arteries, causes (in rare cases) fibrillation of the spleen, and generally shortens the life span. "We strongly recommend," they conclude, "that those interested in good health engage in twenty minutes of sex before breakfast instead."

But such grim warnings little prevail. So the next time a panting jogger pounds by, don't say patronizingly, "Poor guy, he doesn't know what he's missing." Instead, raise your glass in a toast to "a short life and a merry one." For he's just another gay moth who lives but for the pleasure of the moment and cares not for the yawning chasm of the grave.

Of course it is not only men who have lost interest in sex. Allow me to refer you to the dismal findings in *The Journal of Sexual Research* that a survey of 235 married couples indicated more wives (26 percent) enjoyed sex than enjoyed "sewing for leisure" (25 percent). Needless to say, a far greater number (37 percent) preferred reading to either activity, although we can presume this depends on the book. The survey also showed that more men (45 percent) claimed in their macho fashion that they liked sex better than anything, even watching television, which leaves us with 55 percent who don't. But why sex should edge out sewing among women is difficult to comprehend. Sewing, after all, is a calm, restful, highly productive pursuit and afterward, if you haven't made a mistake, you have something to show for it. Sex is precisely the opposite.

I therefore took my own survey to discover the reasons behind this phenomenon and thus advance the pursuit of human knowledge. Women, I quickly found, prefer sex not only to sewing but to a number of other chores about the house, including folding the laundry (especially fitted sheets) (3 percent) and "cleaning out the closet with the cleaning things in it" (0.4 percent). As I suspected, the only criticism most women voiced about sex was that it was unproductive. That helps explain the popularity of reading, for it's quite possible to read and do other things at the same time.

"There's nothing I enjoy more than curling up with a good book and my husband, Richard," says Nancy G. "As for Richard, he likes watching football. So we have lots of activity on Monday nights. In fact, I do find it difficult sometimes keeping my place in the exciting spots."

"In the book?"

"No, in the football game."

And there is hope for sewing, too. Just recently, Mrs. Elizabeth M., after six months of trial and error, successfully managed to combine both activities. "The beginner should confine herself to simple basting," she suggests, "and progress slowly through straight stitching to zig-zagging and lazy daisies. Don't worry about making mistakes at first, although I must say George was none too happy the night I pinch pleated his pajama tops to my new shantung dining room drapes."

"Any particular helpful tips?" I asked.

"Yes," she said, "be sure to thread the needle before you begin."

Thus we see that with a little ingenuity, sex need not be the waste of time that all too many women find it. What is required is merely proper organization and careful planning of the daily duties. Some chores obviously don't combine readily with sex—painting the mail box, for example, or dipping sheep. But, if you put your mind to it, you'll be surprised how many projects you can accomplish at once and sex will remain an enjoyable pursuit for millions of housewives everywhere. Well, 26 percent.

This is not to say that men don't have their problems, too. My friend Hanratty has had some difficulty reconciling his sex life with Catholicism. His problem is not due to lack of devoutness; it's due to lack of understanding.

"Pope John Paul II is a fine man and I know he's wondrous wise," says Hanratty, "because when he gets on the subject of sex, I cannot for the life of me make head nor tail of a word he says. Some great leaders use words I can't understand; His Holiness uses whole paragraphs I can't understand. You remember when he caused all that fuss by saying a man can commit adultery in his heart by looking at his wife in a lustful way? I see that in the paper at breakfast and I say to the Missus, 'Norma,' I say, 'I want you to know that not once in the past twenty-seven years have I looked at you and felt the least bit of lust in my heart.' You would think she would be proud to be married to such a good, upstanding Catholic. Instead, she slaps two waffles on my plate and doesn't speak to me for a week. So when His Holiness comes out with another pro-

nouncement on the subject, I handle it very, very carefully. 'Norma,' I say to the Missus at breakfast, 'the paper
says the pope has decided it is okay for you and me to be
spontaneous.'

" 'Spontaneous how?' she says suspiciously.

" 'Maybe I better read you what he says,' says I. 'He
says, and I quote, "Sometimes it is asserted that ethical
consideration remove spontaneity from the erotic area of
human conduct. But those who accept the ethos proposed
by Christ are still called to the full and mature spontaneity of the relationship that arises from the attraction of
masculinity and femininity."

" 'What's that mean?' says the Missus.

" 'The pope only knows,' says I. 'But I think it means I
don't have to give up my Wednesday night bowling
league once a month any more. Not that I'm complaining,
mind you. For twenty-seven years, I seen my duty and I
done it.'

" 'Your duty?' says she with a scowl.

" 'It is the duty of the pope and the good fathers to
propagate the faith,' says I. 'And it is the duty of us good
laymen to propagate the faithful. With eight fine children,
we can hold our heads up in any parish. But now the pope
says we can do it any time we want.'

" 'You mean just for fun?' says the Missus incredu-
lously.

" 'Sounds like it,' says I.

" 'After twenty-seven years and eight kids,' says she,
'now he tells us.'

"But it don't work out so good," adds Hanratty. "Seems

like the only time the Missus feels spontaneous is when I drag myself home from the plant in a record heat wave. And when I'm feeling spontaneous, she's got a spontaneous urge to wax the whatnot. It's just not likely for two folks to feel spontaneous at the same time spontaneously." Hanratty sighed. "Of course, maybe I got the pope all wrong. I don't know. I tell you, though, if I wasn't worried about saving my immortal soul, I'd become a High Church Episcopalian."

"You think they have a better attitude toward sex?" I asked.

"I hear tell," said Hanratty, "that they don't bother with it at all."

This is certainly not true. Many High Episcopalians are rich, and it is the rich who are constantly being immortalized in the blackest daily ink for their astounding sexual shenanigans. How vividly I recall commenting on this to the noted author Scott F. Fitzgerald: "The rich are different from you and me," I said.

"Yes," he replied, "they have more time."

I said I didn't know that was the problem.

"It goes to the heart of it," he said. "You take the poor man. If he's lucky, he's laboring eight hours a day in the foundry and moonlighting at the pizza parlor bagging pepperonis to make ends meet. Or, more likely, he's standing in line at the unemployment office, the free medical clinic, or his friendly neighborhood bus stop. It's no wonder we never read about his sex life in the *National Enquirer.*"

"He's more moral than a rich man?"

"Certainly. If he's in tip-top shape, he may be able to devote ten minutes a week to blind, raging passion without falling asleep. And his wife is probably too tired to give a hoot."

"But the rich have more time?"

"That's what money buys. Take a typical rich man. He rises at noon, calls his broker, and his work is over for the day. He never stands in line, not for an unemployment check, a food stamp, or a bus. In fact, there are people in this country so rich they have doctors who make house calls."

"Amazing, if true," I said. "And time leads to sex?"

"No, it leads to boredom. There's Robert and Theodore and Caroline and Alicia in the solarium. 'What do you want to do, Theodore?' says Robert, yawning.

" 'Oh, I don't know,' says Theodore with a lethargic shrug. 'What about . . .'

" 'We did that eight times before breakfast,' says Caroline, wrinkling her nose.

" 'Well,' says Alicia without much enthusiasm, 'I suppose we could always . . .'

" 'Might as well,' agrees Robert with a sigh. 'But dibs on sado.'

"And the first thing they know," concluded Fitzgerald, "they're plastered all over page one."

"Disgusting," I said. "Is there no hope of rescuing these wretched overprivileged from their sordid lives?"

Fitzgerald said he had high hopes for a new program called Workfare for the Rich. The basic premise, he said, was that a rich person receives far more government assistance these days than a poor person. So enterprise zones would be established in such ghettoes of unemployment as Bel Air and Palm Beach, where any resident who wished to continue receiving tax breaks on unearned income and the like would have to take a job. I asked what unskilled rich people could do.

"We're confident they could be trained for simple ghetto tasks like polishing trophies, mowing polo fields, stitching little alligators on shirts, and stuffing quail," he said.

"I say you can't solve problems by throwing money at them," I said. "The rich made their beds, let them lie in them or whatever it is they do wherever it is they do it."

"You have to be more tolerant," he said. "Remember the great wisdom of Abraham Lincoln: 'If the Good Lord didn't love rich people, he wouldn't have created Reaganomics.' "

"You could say the same for poor people," I said.

Fitzgerald nodded. "Them, too," he agreed.

This takes care of the rich and the poor. What about the rest of us stolidly married folk? Think back on the first encounter with your beloved. Recall the rush of blood at the first touch, the heart-pounding joy of the first kiss, the angel-singing ecstasy of oneness during the first intimate act. . . .

(If the reader will forgive me, I plan to avoid using the phrase "sexual intercourse" at all costs. Unfortunately, I happened to be present at Maxime's the night Muffie B. shocked the world by being caught *in flagrante delicto* on top of the table with her date, the Marquis de S., after the waiter had taken away the *Oie Braisée aux Marrons* in order to make room for the *Gateau de Crepes à la Normande*. "*Mon Dieu*, Madame!" cried the sommelier, rushing up, "What do you think you are doing?" Muffie gazed on him coolly. "We are engaged," she said, "in sexual intracourse." I therefore cannot use the phrase, or anything resembling it, without thinking of *Oie Braisée aux Marrons*, which gives me indigestion.)

In any event, once two playthings of passion are wed, what happens to their insatiable desire to engage in whatever-it-is-you-want-to-call-it? The answer, I'm afraid, is that sex after wedlock is like shooting fish in a barrel. Gone are the thrills of the chase, the intriguing uncertainty of the outcome, and the final triumph of the kill. Instead, either both of you are willing or one of you isn't, and that's that. The truth of this theorem was brought home to me the day my dear wife, Glynda, and I heard an eminent cardiologist analyze the subject on the car radio: "I see nothing wrong with a man who's had a heart attack having sex," he said, "but only with his wife." "There, you see!" cried Glynda happily for, as founding president of the International Wives Union, she heartily welcomes any evidence of the virtues of marital fidelity. But after an instant's thought, the joy fled from her face. "Oh, no," she muttered.

It is in crises like these that we good husbands can be counted upon. I reached over and patted her knee. "If I had a heart attack," I said, "I'd only have sex with anyone *but* you."

Her reaction to this comforting remark just showed how

far she was beyond solace. For the cardiologist's opinion
that there is exciting sex after marriage, if not with your
spouse, seems to be widely held. Where there is a recognized problem in our society today, there are a spate of
books and magazine articles on how to deal with it. But
does such advice help? The answer is a resounding,
"You're darned tootin!" The proof is in an article I came
across in *The Ladies Home Companion* by Giselda Garch, an
obvious *nom de plume*. It is entitled, "How Advice on How
to Save My Marriage Saved My Marriage." The text fol-
lows:

I guess it was reading "Has That Special Glint Gone
Out of Your Hubby's Eye?" in your issue of last Jan-
uary that started it. I realized then that for ten years
Fred had come home every evening with open arms
which he used to get two beers out of the refrigerator
before settling down to read his paper. So I followed
the advice in the article. Each night for a week I threw
my arms around him at the door while wearing nothing but whipped cream. This made both the milkman
and dry cleaners happy. Not Fred, though. He seems
to be growing a mite testier as he gets older.

I could see that more drastic steps were required.
Having read "Take an Interest in Your Husband's
Work" in the February issue, I took an interest in his
work. "What do you do for a living, Fred?" I asked
him straight out at breakfast. "I work," he explained,
rattling his paper. I felt it was a start.

So in order to "Make Yourself a More Interesting
Person" (March), I took an adult education course in
Urban Redevelopment and a tab of LSD before din-

ner. Fred didn't seem much interested in urban redevelopment but he couldn't take his eyes off me as I
stood on the couch sharpening the hedge shears. Now I
was making progress. In April, I enthusiastically took
to heart the advice to "Never Bother Hubby with
Household Problems." I didn't bother him with the
dry rot in the kitchen floor. I think I may have seen
that special glint in his eye when his leg went through.
Perhaps it was his delight in not spilling a drop from
either can of beer.

Yet had I done all I could? I hadn't. It was while
reading, "To Save Your Marriage, Have an Affair" in
May that I resolved to make the supreme sacrifice. I
broke the news to him as gently as possible. ("Be honest," the article said.) "To be honest, Fred," I said, "I
am running off to Duluth to have an affair with your
best friend, Harville." I must say he took this thunder-
bolt very well. "What are best friends for?" he said.

For two weeks in the Bide-an-Hour Motel in Duluth, I did my best to make Fred happy. And it
worked! "It was only to make you happy, Fred," I told
him on my return.

And there, at last, was unquestionably that special
glint in his eye. "To be honest," he said, "I've never
been happier."

So that's how advice on how to save your marriage
saved my marriage. The only question I now have—
and I think this must run through the minds of many
readers of your fine magazine—is what the hell am I
going to do with it?

From this, we can see that the practice of adultery has
become widely accepted, if not in my house. As confession

is always good for somebody-or-other's soul, I must admit that I once did make an irrevocable decision to have an affair. I remember the moment vividly. We were at the breakfast table and dear Glynda had just handed me a bowl containing a three-minute egg and one piece of dry whole-wheat toast.

"I didn't ask for a three-minute egg and one piece of dry whole-wheat toast," I said a trifle irritably.

"But you *always* have a three-minute egg and one piece of dry whole-wheat toast," said Glynda.

So I decided there and then to have an affair because Glynda, as usual, was right. "Life is more than a three-minute egg and one piece of dry whole-wheat toast," I said to myself. "To be richly textured and joyously worth living, life must be crammed with excitement, intrigue, and heart-pounding adventure." But which of the three billion women on this planet should I choose as my inamorata? How old should this creature of my dreams be? How young? How svelte? How fleshily plump? How willowy? How petite? I debated these burning questions for a good ten seconds before picking the one beautiful woman who I knew would be good for me. "Please pass the salt, Glynda," I said, "and do you want to have an affair?"

I suppose I will be faulted by the sophisticated for not wooing Glynda more seductively. Some might say I should have begun my romantic campaign by bringing her flowers. But I never bring Glynda flowers. When I bring Glynda flowers, she sniffs them suspiciously, looks up at me from under a wary frown and says, "What have you done wrong?" That's why I don't bring Glynda flowers. Thus I wasn't surprised that when I asked Glynda to have an affair she looked up at me from under a wary frown. "What have you done wrong?" she said. "It's the car, isn't it? I know it's the car."

I exercised all my powers of persuasion to convince her that (1) the car was fine and that (2) we could, as a married couple, have all the excitement, intrigue, and adventure of an affair with none of the attendant risks and heartaches. I'm not quite sure I did convince her of the latter but she finally agreed to have an "intimate little dinner" with me at Le Boudoir. "Anything for a dinner out" is how she phrased her maidenly acceptance. "I'll meet you in front."

"No, no," I said, "let's meet just inside the door. We must protect your reputation."

She gave me another one of those looks. "How did you know that's the way to do it?" she said.

"Intuition! Intuition!" I explained.

Le Boudoir was as intimate as a romantic heart could desire: pink napery and crystal, paintings of topless shepherdesses on the walls, and candles so dim that you couldn't, thank heaven, read the prices on the menu. "Ah, yes, m'sieu," said the head waiter suavely, "the table in the corner."

"Come here often?" asked Glynda sweetly.

"I found it in a restaurant guide under 'Intimate Little Supper Spots,' " I said. "Would you care for the *Escargot avec Aphrodisiaque?*" I then went all out ordering this and that, spouting little pleasantries, taking her hand in mine, and even gazing deeply into her eyes which I hadn't gazed deeply into since our honeymoon. But all to little avail. "Have I done something wrong?" I finally asked.

"I just can't stand seeing you enjoy having an affair so much," she said.

But I persisted, *"Voulez-vous,"* I whispered over the espresso, *"coucher avec moi?"*

"Where did you pick up that kind of language?" she asked.

"I'll never forget my high-school French," I said.

She managed a grin. "Okay," she said. "But will you remember my name in the morning?"

By the time I had the fire burning in the living room, Frank Sinatra crooning on the record player, and two brandies poured, she decided to slip into something more comfortable. But first, she said, she wanted to take off the gardenia I had so boldly given her and float it in a bowl of water. She waved demurely as she headed for the kitchen. How exciting! How intriguing! How adventurous! How long could we keep this up? As though in answer to my unspoken question, Glynda's lovely voice came wafting down the hall. "Do something!" it said. "The darned garbage disposal is backed up again."

So I do feel that any affair I have in the foreseeable future will have to be catered. For I've decided that what I *really* want in life is a three-minute egg and one piece of dry whole-wheat toast. But for those others of you out there who are still intrigued with the possibilities of what sociologists refer to as "hanky-panky," it should be mentioned that having a real affair is not as easy as it sounds. Let me cite just one case history from my voluminous files:

Case History Number 67842-e

Subjects: JASON AND LINDA PANGROVE

Jason Pangrove was thirty-two years old when, driven by man's insatiable lust for challenge and adventure, he decided to have an affair. Having an affair, however, posed three serious problems. The first was to find a young woman of like mind. Jason wasn't about to have an affair with just anybody. His mistress-to-be, he decided after grave thought, must have discretion, intelligence, wit, charm, and an ample bosom. As Miss Chard in Payroll so clearly fulfilled the fifth condition, he was confident she would measure up in the other four.

"Miss Chard," he began on cornering her by the coffee machine, "would you like to have . . ."

"I thought you were a married man, Mr. Pangrove," said Miss Chard.

". . . the United Nations arbitrate the Monrovia–South Yemen border dispute?" finished Jason hastily.

He quickly discovered a surprising number of young women who weren't interested in wasting their unmarried years on married men. Even as he searched, a second serious problem began to gnaw at his mind: If he ever did find a young woman willing to help him practice infidelity, where would he find the time? For Jason had a nine-twenty-to-four-forty government job which left him little room for maneuver. Worse, he couldn't very well tell Linda he was working late as no one in the history of the civil service has ever worked late. So if he arrived home for dinner at some ungodly hour he would have to come up with a highly imaginative excuse, such as being treed by an escaped hippopotamus. But he couldn't possibly get treed three nights a week. Linda would suspect.

Lastly, if he did somehow find the target and the time, where would he find the money? Even in these liberated times, he assumed he would have to pop for half the wine and roses. He couldn't very well put a room at The Wine and Roses Motel on his Master Card. This would require giving the clerk his right name and, when the bill came in, Linda the right explanation. Then, too, what about Christmas presents, birthday presents and, as the years rolled by, anniversary presents? Moreover, come to think of it, what about remembering all these new dates along with remembering all the old dates that he kept forgetting? And there was always the problem of running into somebody you knew; or somebody becoming crotchety; or somebody becoming hysterical; or somebody becoming, for God's sakes, pregnant. Pregnant? Jesus Christ!

In the end, Jason quelled his lust for challenge and adventure by taking up golf. He even had trouble explaining *that* to Linda.

I should probably also deal with the question of sex for hire. I'd be glad to. In fact, I dealt with it just the other day. I was idly leafing through the Yellow Pages looking for an escrow company when I stumbled on "Escort Services—Personal." Here, before my startled eyes, were no fewer than thirty-four pages depicting a myriad of supplicating young maidens, all of whom very much wanted to be my personal escort. There was Carol and Julie; Carol (no relation) and Jenny; Kay and Linda; Diane and Erica; Donna, Jill, Chris, and Linda (no relation); Lisa and Julie (no relation); and so on and so on. All were seductively attractive; most had long, ironed hair; and each was obviously eager to guarantee, as did "Oui Girls," my "complete satisfaction," which is certainly good to know if you're looking for an escort to take to the flicks.

As an old married man, I wasn't one bit tempted. NOT ONE BIT. But I was, of course, curious to find out how much escorts cost these days. I'm always getting asked the cost of all sorts of things at cocktail parties. I had trouble making up my mind whom to call. "Flaming Desire" sounded interesting. "Innocence" struck me as intriguingly kinky. And I did like the large-lettered advice in the half-page ad for "Danielle's Specialties." It said simply: "DO IT!" In the end, being somewhat reticent, I settled for Donna & Karen, two straight-haired blondes who offered "x-tra special service" in return for Visa and Master Card.

The lady who answered the phone said the cost of an escort was $60 an hour, which would rule out escorting her to see *War and Peace,* plus a tip. And how much was the tip? "Between $60 and $100," said the lady. "It's negotiable. But we do accept Visa and MasterCard."

I could see Donna or Karen (I'm not fussy) gazing deeply into my eyes. I could see her reach into the bosom of her low-cut gown to take out her credit card machine and blank forms. I could see my dear wife, Glynda, going through the bills and asking, "What's this $150 for Donna & Karen's X-tra Special Service?"

Thus, as I say, I wasn't one bit tempted, all things considered, and I decided to have a cold shower instead. When I came out, there was Mordred fiddling with the Yellow Pages.

"What are you doing, Mordred?" I demanded.

"I'm letting my fingers do the walking, Dad," he said.

"Go wash your hands," I said.

So, as you may well have surmised, I am a firm upholder of marital fidelity because (1) it is the decent, rational course to pursue in life and (2) I know what's good for me. Propounding the cause of monogamy, however, has not always been easy. I recall suggesting to a young friend back in the sixties that he have a go at monogamy. "Monogamy?" he said. "Is that where you get tied down on a dining room table?" But in recent years, I do believe it's making an awesome comeback. While monogamists may miss the thrill of the chase and the joy of the kill, they enjoy such munificent rewards as not having to ask anyone's name on awakening in the morning, not having to undergo the dread trauma of rejection, and not having to adjust to the whims of some stranger who may insist on sleeping with his or her feet on your pillow. And, at the end of the evening, when one monogamist says to the other, "Our place or our place?" the issue is rarely in doubt. So I say, "Down with promiscuity!" As Dorothy Parker pithily, if inelegantly, put it long ago, "The screwing you get isn't worth the screwing you get."

Therefore, we see that the entire issue of how often a

couple sleeps together after marriage boils down to the question of whether or not they have a double bed. This is a question that concerns every American from the corner newspaper vendor to the president of our great land. As it happens, I have made one of the few studies extant of the sleeping habits of our presidents. This has been a matter of abiding interest to all Americans for more than two hundred years. Observe all the signs today which boast that "George Washington Slept Here." You will note that he slept there without the company of Mrs. Washington. He was definitely not a double bed man and the fact that he was The Father of Our Country and no one else speaks well for the planned parenthood technique known as "geographical birth control." In our own times, President and Mrs. Kennedy set an example by sleeping in separate bedrooms and I always felt that if only the peasants of Bangladesh and other third-world nations had seen fit to emulate them, it would have gone a long way toward snuffing out the population explosion. Little is known about the sleeping habits of Mr. Nixon, a secretive soul, except that he always slept with his necktie on. But it was President and Mrs. Ford who stirred the country by publicly announcing that they slept, by golly, in a double bed and were proud of it. And I must say that the thought of the ebullient Mr. Ford parking his gum on the bedpost and climbing under the covers with that attractive Mrs. Ford was enough to send my blood pounding.

So if presidents can reveal their intimate sleeping arrangements, I see no reason to withhold mine from a curious public: My dear wife, Glynda, and I sleep in a double bed. We always have and, I fear, we always will. For the truth of the matter is that no one—no man, woman, or child in this great country of ours—likes to sleep in a double bed. Getting into a double bed on a cold evening can be a richly rewarding experience. Waking up in a double bed on a Saturday or Sunday morning can create an ambience of luxurious indolence. But *sleeping* in a double bed? No sane human being could possibly contend that the weird custom of two people sharing the same bed is conducive to sleep. Why, then, you may well ask, do so many Americans attempt to sleep in double beds? The answer, once again, is cowardice.

When Glynda and I were married, we couldn't wait to sleep, or whatever, in a double bed. It was the initial purchase for our nest. First of all, it was far cheaper than twin beds, and every penny counted. More importantly, it announced to the world that we were so madly in love with each other that we couldn't bear being more than several inches apart even when we were unconscious. It was this latter aspect of double beds that dear Glynda, who publicly takes the romantic view of marriage, seized upon at the time and hasn't let go of until this day. And I must say that when you are poor and romantic and young enough to sleep soundly through the night, a double bed offers advantages. For one thing, it teaches the art of compromise on such major issues as the firmness of the mattress, the number of blankets, and when to turn the reading light off:

"That light doesn't bother me a bit, dear, even though I do have a little headache, but don't you think you should turn it out and get some sleep? For your own good?"

"I will, dear, just as soon as I figure out how we're going to pay this little bill you ran up at the Bon Marche for our new eiderdown quilt."

But conditions change. Glynda and I are no longer young nor particularly poor. Unfortunately, as I say, Glynda, as president of the International Wives Union, clings to romanticism and how on earth do you tell the woman you've sworn to love, honor, and cherish that you want to kick her out of your bed?

Over the years, I've made strenuous, if subtle, efforts in this direction. As soon as we were rich enough to make hotel reservations I would ask the clerk, if Glynda wasn't listening, for twin beds. Oh, how I would look forward to a good night's sleep! When we arrived, Glynda would pretend dismay at the sight of the eighteen-inch abyss that yawned between us, although I always suspected she was by then as secretly pleased by the prospect as I.

"Oh, look," she would say, "They gave us twin beds!"

"Yes," I would lie like a trooper, "they didn't have a single double in the house."

And it was only this summer that I finally got our sleeping bags apart. Each July we repair to our cabin at Lake Algae. As the cabin offers no double beds, my first assigned task has always been to push two cots together and zip our two sleeping bags into one. Given the ridge between the cot mattresses and the coziness of zipped-together sleeping bags, I have never considered the cabin at Lake Algae much of a vacation. This summer I finally rebelled. I pushed the two cots together as always, but I defiantly rolled out our two sleeping bags separately, one a good three inches from the other. Glynda viewed the arrangement thoughtfully. "Well, all right," she finally said. "But what will the children say?"

And now aren't those of you who asked if there was sex after marriage glad that you did?

CHAPTER FOUR

The Seven Marital Sins

A S AN EXPERT on marriage, I have long urged a drastic tightening of the nation's divorce laws. In all too many states, the bonds of matrimony can be severed for specious, if not downright frivolous, reasons. The American nuclear family will continue to be in danger of imminent explosion until the grounds for divorce are limited to the seven major causes of marital breakups and/or justifiable homicides. These are:

INDOMINABLE WILL POWER

Every study shows that the ability to reject food, drink, and tobacco in the presence of a spouse who cannot is the leading factor in the increasing number of broken homes. Before you announce that you just love cheesecake, but you're on a diet, ask yourself whether the three hundred calories you'll save is worth the marriage you'll lose. A case in point is that of Emily Harmsworthy of Sarasota, Florida. Mrs. Harmsworthy displayed her indominable will power by going on and sticking to the Calcutta Regimen, which required her to renounce smoking, drinking, and eating anything other than four tablespoons of boiled bulgur a day. Like anyone with indominable will power, Mrs. Harmsworthy felt irresistibly compelled to extol its virtues to all who would listen, particularly her husband, George. "You really could do it if you'd only try," she would tell George as she turned down a first helping of chocolate mousse. In two weeks, as any knowledgeable observer could have foretold, Mrs. Harmsworthy lost her bloodshot eyes, her spare tire, and 17 pounds—the 172 pounds being her husband, George, who now lives in Cocoa Palms with an overweight taxi dancer.

Courage in the Face of Adversity

This covers a wide gamut of sins, ranging from the all-too-familiar spouse who stoically insists on helping with the dishes although running a temperature of 103.6° and covered with small red spots to the insufferable helpmate (usually male) who gamely shouts, "Come on, kiddo, do you want to live forever!" as he flips his skis over the edge and plunges down the headwall into the teeth of a raging blizzard.

In this respect, I recall Glynda's and my first flight across the Atlantic. Glynda is a somewhat nervous flier, and I have scars on my wrists, which she grasps with incredible strength on take-offs and landings, to prove it. We had arrived at the airport two hours early as Glynda always likes to throw a farewell party for the two of us in the cocktail lounge before boarding. I enjoy a festive farewell party as well as the next man, but as our flight was at 9:00 A.M., I was a bit testy by the time we had taken our seats. Glynda had asked the flight attendant the usual questions, such as, "Is the pilot a family man?" (they all are), and we began to taxi out to the runway. "What's that quinch-quinch-quinch noise?" inquired Glynda, drawing blood from just above my wristwatch.

I favored her with a patronizing, masculine chuckle. "Just the normal sounds any aircraft makes," I said, enjoying her silly feminine fears. "I've heard it dozens of times."

The aircraft stopped. "Bad news, folks," said the pilot in a fair imitation of a Chuck Yeager drawl. "Seems like we're going to have to head back to the terminal seeing as how we've got an iddy-biddy fire in old number two."

Glynda gave me a look that melted any courage I had left in the face of adversity. Now when she hears strange noises on aircraft, I cooperate fully by closing my eyes and saying, "Let us pray."

UNDAUNTED CHEERFULNESS

Common symptoms here include jumping out of bed or making any other sudden moves before breakfast, whistling before lunch, saying "Have a nice day" on Mondays, or delivering cheery comments like "Don't fret, dear; anyone could have a vapor lock here in the fast lane of the Santa Ana Freeway."

UNMITIGATED HELPFULNESS

The problem with unmitigatedly helpful spouses is not that they are usually wrong but that they are usually right. In this regard, clinical psychologists are fond of citing the case of Heather Beardsley of Four Corners, Iowa, who was canning peaches in the spring of 1984 while her husband, Carl, was out in the backyard working on the power mower. Mr. Beardsley had been attempting to start the device of one hour and fourteen minutes when Mrs. Beardsley, on her way to the garage for more Mason jars, thoughtlessly asked, "Is it plugged in?" As Mrs. Beardsley later told friends, "I was certainly lucky it wasn't a chain saw."

INTELLECTUAL PROWESS

This includes knowing the seven-letter word (across) for the medieval ancestor of the glockenspiel, how to pronounce *chaise longue,* and not merely that it takes ten points to bid two clubs over one spade but saying so out loud. This quality is often exacerbated by a preference for silent German movies to football on television or, for that matter, television.

Here, again, the heart of the problem is being right. And, while I am confessing my own sins, I must confess this is one of mine. As the old saw goes, I thought I was mistaken once in 1954, but I was wrong. God knows, I've done my best over the years to disguise this fatal flaw in my character. For example, when I know for a certainty that Rome fell to the barbarians in 476 A.D., I would never dream of saying "I know for a certainty that Rome fell to the barbarians in 476 A.D." What I defensively say instead is "I think maybe Rome may possibly have fallen to the barbarians perhaps sometime around 476 A.D. or so, give or take a couple of hundred years." Even so, I fear there are times Glynda finds me insufferable. But that's the punishment God has inflicted on those of us who are handicapped in life by always being right. ·

STEADFAST UNSELFISHNESS

Here we have the spouse who invariably takes the burnt toast, orders the cheapest dish on the menu, refuses to buy new clothes, and often says, "Why don't you go see what's on tv while I just run a few things through the dishwasher?"

The sole goal in life of the spouse who is steadfastly unselfish, of course, is to inflict unbearable guilt feelings on the spouse who is not. Steadfastly unselfish spouses should be treated with tolerance and forgiveness. For example, when Glynda says to me, "Go ahead, you take those last few kernels of popcorn; I'm stuffed," I should simply reply, "I forgive you." I should, but why start a fight?

UNFLAGGING HONESTY

Res ipsa loquitor. If there is one sin no marriage can survive, it is unflagging honesty. You might be able to get away with "Better check, dear, I think the waiter gave you too much change"; or even "You're right, by golly, you *are* putting on a little pot." If you'd care to sample the joys of a single life, however, try "Yes, she (or he) is more attractive, intelligent and witty than you, but what can we possibly do about that?"

By narrowing the grounds for divorce to these seven major causes, we will not only save thousands of marriages annually but we will also unclutter our overburdened judicial system. As it stands now, our courts are jammed with petty disputes over such matters as chronic infidelity, the squandering of joint bank accounts, and unexplained seven-year absences. These minor irritants to a happy marriage, I strongly feel, could better be resolved by shouting.

CHAPTER FIVE

The Critical Need for Sympathy in Marriage & How to Get All That You Can

MARRIAGE IS a competition in suffering. You should plant this firmly in your mind as you walk back down the aisle and climb in the car to go off on your honeymoon. This is the time to test the marital waters and establish yourself as an experienced and dedicated sufferer. I would suggest some such remark as "I can't wait to get to bed; I hardly slept a wink last night."

Sleep, you will find, is one of the principal battlegrounds in competitive suffering. It poses a grave challenge to the neophyte for you must be alert and on your toes the instant your eyes flutter open each morning so that you can leap into the fray sounding properly haggard. For the first question you must face every marital day is: "How did you sleep?" The proper response is "Fine, just fine," as you add with a sigh, "once I finally managed to doze off."

Here, you will be asked what time that was. At this point, you may wish to attempt The Sunrise Gambit: "Oh, about 5:16 A.M., I guess. It was just getting light out and I happened to notice that sunrise was at 5:33 today."

This sounds simple but if you are up against a seasoned veteran, The Sunrise Gambit is sure to draw The Barking Dog Response: "Oh, then you must have heard that darned dog barking, too." Now you are faced with the dilemma of whether there really was a barking dog (you can't trust anybody in this business) and, if so, at what hour and how long it barked. Probably the most effective way out of this trap is to exclaim, "Is that smoke I smell?" Should you make the error of inquiring instead how your spouse slept, you might have to deal with The Snoring Riposte, for which there's no known defense. "Oh, not too badly," comes the deadly thrust, "except that your snoring kept me awake."

This brings us—quickly, if you have your wits about you—to: "How do you feel?" Again, the proper reply is a cheery, "Fine, just fine." But if you are on the replying end, resist the temptation to then clutch your chest and keel over as this is a hard act to follow. Instead, settle for something more mundane like a hacking cough, a near-terminal wheeze, and a whispered, "I think my cold is better."

If you are dealing with a world-class sufferer, this will probably get you: "Yes, you seem to be getting over yours much faster than I got over mine," followed by a twist of the knife: "But do take good care of yourself. I got up much too soon because your relatives were coming, and I still have these dreadful pains right through here." After an exchange like that, you at least won't have to ask how your spouse feels.

So off to breakfast. Thrust: "Oh, just lemon juice and water for me; I can't seem to lose a pound." Parry: "I know what you mean. All day yesterday, the only things that crossed my lips were three tangerine rinds and seven alfalfa sprouts."

Breakfast, too, is a good time to discuss the children and which one of you suffers from them most: "I'm so worried about Malphasia. Did you speak to her about not moving in with that New Wave electric sitar player?"

"No, I've been much too concerned that Mordred will develop irreversible brain damage if he continues watching 'Monday Night Football.' "

You must now decide whether you wish to suffer over anticipated suffering. Do so only on days that provide worthwhile events. A dental appointment is always a worthwhile event. "He's going to go into that tender bicuspid, darn it, and you know I can't stand Novocaine."

The time finally comes to go your separate ways. After you do, be sure to take notes of all the little happenings during your day that could brighten your evening. These might include: the bus that passed you up, how Higgens in Marketing dumped the Hempstead file on you; who kept you waiting how long for what even though you've been a customer there for seven years; and, if you are incredibly lucky, the swinging door that banged into you, severely spraining your right wrist.

A word should be said here about suffering from physical causes. Never, under any circumstances, mention that you are suffering. Suffering by itself is not enough. You only get credit for suffering nobly. For example, if I did sprain my wrist, I wouldn't dream of telling Glynda. Instead, I'd wrap it in an elastic bandage and roll up my shirt sleeve before pouring her evening martini. Similarly, should I slice my finger while she was in another room, I would stanch the flow with a paper towel which I would leave on the counter top to greet her on her return. "Oh, it's just a scratch," I'd say in answer to her inescapable query. "But perhaps I'd better put a Band-Aid on it so I don't bleed all over the rug." Yes, sir, stoicism is the key to marital suffering. Be brave, be noble, be stoic, and be darned sure your partner discovers just how brave, noble, and stoic you are.

So, with all this in mind, have a lousy day, worrisome kids, a defective digestive track, a chronic cold, a painful injury, endemic insomnia, and a very, very happy marriage.

CHAPTER SIX ———

Togetherness

A S PRESIDENT OF the International Wives'
Union, Glynda believes wholeheartedly in Togetherness.
It is the union's credo that married folks, in order to demonstrate to the world their burning love for each other,
should strive to spend every possible moment together for
the remainder of their natural lives. This is not the union's
only purpose, of course. Actually, its prime function is to
side with the wife in any divorce case. For the husband is
automatically guilty until proven innocent and that'll be
the day. Its members are also sworn to report any faintly
suspicious behavior on the part of any other member's
husband, solely for that member's "own good," and all
have vowed never to provide an attractive dinner partner
for any husband visiting town without his spouse.

But Glynda focuses on Togetherness. Indeed, I have often dreamed of at last being chosen the first hero astronaut to be sent to the far reaches of the universe where no man has ever gone before. There I'll stand in front of the gleaming rocket, strapping on my helmet in the glare of the television lights. And there, standing beside me, strapping on her helmet, will be Glynda, demanding to know how I got us into this.

Actually, we are not alone. Most marriages, I've found, are initially based on Togetherness. Typical was that of Newton and Phyllis Phisch. When first wed, they couldn't bear being out of each other's sight. The Phisches did everything together. They marched down the aisle of the supermarket together, his hand over hers on the handle of the shopping cart. They did the laundry at the laundromat together, her head on his shoulder as they watched his socks tumble playfully in the drier with her kerchief. And, much to the amazement of every seasoned couple of their acquaintance, they talked to each other at cocktail parties.

This orgy of oneness lasted four years. One night, Newt put down *Crime and Punishment,* which they had been reading aloud to each other, and sighed. "Now what'll we do?" he asked, scratching his chest thoughtfully. "We've already picked the spider mites off the ceanothus together, memorized all the trivial answers in Trivial Pursuit together, and built an Eiffel Tower out of swizzle sticks together."

"Stop scratching, dear," said Phyllis. "We can always chat together."

"Okay," said Newt. "You first."

"Well ..." said Phyllis. There was a good minute of dead silence. They looked at each other blankly. The awful truth dawned: After four long years of constant Togetherness, they had inexorably, inevitably, and finally run out things to say to each other. Could this marriage be saved? Yes! It was Newt who saved it. "Darling," he said, "we must obviously recharge our marital batteries. I will sacrifice myself and become a bachelor for one whole week, though I may perish from loneliness without you."

"That's most thoughtful of you, dear," said Phyllis. "For I think if I heard you mispronounce 'Raskolnikov' one more time, I'd scream."

So Newt went off to the Excelsior Hotel, where he read in bed with his shoes on, scratched anywhere he wanted to, and didn't eat one single leafy green vegetable for an entire week. As for Phyllis, she laughed aloud at her own jokes, napped in the bathtub, and whistled a lot through her teeth.

When Newt returned, a new life awaited them. They read the paper separately at breakfast, attended alone the movies that each preferred, and carefully rationed their conversation, knowing now how precious each word was. Just the other day, they were named Most Devoted Couple of the Year.

I couldn't wait to tell Glynda about the Phisches. "Do you think that I, too, should have a week as a bachelor in order to recharge our marital batteries?" I hesitantly asked her.

And, oh, how my heart soared when she sweetly replied,

"Of course you should, dear." And, oh, how it plummeted earthward when she added, "Where will we go?"

I realize that there are some, including Glynda, who will feel that the Phisches are an extreme case. In this respect, I was pleasantly surprised to read that Jerry Ford, who was one day to become president of the United States of America, took the older kids to a baseball game while his wife, Betty, was giving birth to their youngest child.

"Do you now think you should have demanded he stay home?" *People* magazine's relentless interviewer asked the nation's former first lady.

"Oh, no," replied Mrs. Ford, who has always been my second favorite wife in the whole world, "because I don't believe that when you marry a person you should attempt to change his personality."

She went on to confide that she really loved the big galoot and that she was always glad to see him when he found an opportunity to drop by their retirement home in Palm Springs to say hello. "But there are times," she admitted, "if he's around, say, fourteen days in a row, I begin to wonder whether maybe he ought to be on the road so I can get a little more done."

Talk about your ideal marriages. What tolerance! What compatibility! What efficiency in assigning the tasks in marriage! For Mrs. Ford is obviously better at having babies and Mr. Ford is obviously more qualified to attend baseball games. You have to hand it to those rare couples who have somehow managed to achieve such a high plateau:

"Good morning, Betty," says Jerry, bouncing down the

stairs to breakfast. "Isn't it a beautiful morning? And what are your plans for today?"

"Well, dear," says Betty, blushing modestly, "I thought I just might have a little baby."

"Wonderful! Wonderful!" says Jerry, rubbing his hands. "As I've always said, I think every girl should have a hobby. But why didn't you tell me the good news, you little dickens you?"

"I would have, dear, but you haven't been home for nine months."

"Yes, I guess I have been a bit busy making speeches and doing all the other things a successful politician does. But from now on I'm going to see to it that we do more things together, like . . . like . . . I know! Let's have breakfast!"

"Oh, that would be lovely, dear. And after breakfast, what would you like to do?"

"Me. Oh, it's such a nice day I think I'll take in the baseball game. Say! Would you like to come?"

"No, I think I'll have a little baby instead."

"Oh, that's right. Well, you go right ahead and do what you want. Don't you worry about me. I think I can find my way out to the ballpark all right."

"My goodness, you're so unselfish, Jerry. I don't suppose . . . I don't know quite how to say this . . . Well, I don't suppose you'd like to be nearby when I had my baby, would you?"

"Good gosh, Betty, why? I know as much about having babies as you do about baseball."

"Of course, dear. It was just a silly thought. And it will

do you a world of good to get out. After all, you've been cooped up with me for eight hours now."

"You sure you don't want me to hang around a bit? I don't mind if I miss batting practice."

"No, no, you run along. And have a nice day."

"Thank you. And you have a nice baby."

So it all works out perfectly. Jerry has a nice time at the game and Betty has a nice baby. Then when he gets home two weeks later, they have lots and lots to talk about:

"It was three to two in the bottom of the ninth," says Jerry at the dinner table. "Muldoon's on first . . ."

"Excuse me for interrupting, dear," says Betty, "but don't you want to hear about the baby? It's a beautiful little girl."

"Oh, yeah, that's great. Well, I guess I better hit the road."

"Without waiting for dessert? I've done something to offend you, haven't I, dear?"

"Well, golly, don't you even want to know who won?"

Now there's a marriage made in Heaven—or some other place I'm not familiar with. For, as the Phisches proved, two human beings can communicate with each other only for a limited number of hours before they run out of things to say. After all, there are only a certain number of words in the language and they can only be joined in a certain number of combinations. I'm not sure what the limit is for talking to each other. A hundred thousand hours? A million? But I'm fairly positive that there must be a limit and when that limit is reached, they will be doomed to sit and stare blankly at each other until death doth them part. To postpone this horrible prospect as long as possible, I have long opposed the doctrine of Togetherness, which serves only to throw two people together. In hopes of saving my treasured marriage, I have long espoused such drastic measures as separate vacations and nights out on the town, for me, with the boys—all to little avail. Yet some people do take separate vacations. I asked my friend Barkenthaler how he did it.

"Very carefully," he said. Here is his invaluable advice:

The first problem Xenia and I faced in tackling the matter head on (Barkenthaler began) was how to bring up the subject. Frankly, I think Xenia had been as secretly intrigued as I for years with the thought of our getting away from each other for a week or so. But who has the courage to open a can of adders like that? I would no more come home and say, "Hey, I've got a great idea: Let's take separate vacations!" than I would come home and say, "Hey, I've got a great idea: Let's get a divorce!" In fact, I see no difference between the two statements.

What triggered our joint liberation was an invitation I received in the mail to a Gala Four-Day Stag Reunion of my college glee club. "They're great guys," I told Xenia with all the enthusiasm I could muster. "You'll love meeting them. Oh, I won't sleep until we get there!"

"It says it's stag," said Xenia.

"Stag? Darn, so it does," I said, adding nobly, "Well, I'm certainly not going to go without you."

"No, you go ahead," she said. "I'll stay home and pay bills."

In the end, however, she generously agreed to take a week's cruise in the Caribbean, something she'd never been able to do primarily because I've always said I'd prefer a week in a land-based sanitarium. Thus, amid a flurry of protests concerning who was the most heartbroken at the thought of being apart even for a moment, we each went happily off on our separate vacations.

I will pass over what happened at my gala stag reunion. It was what usually happens at gala stag reunions, and I will simply say that a plea of *nolo contendere* to throwing a piano out a window is not the same as a plea of guilty.

Actually, the vacation itself is no problem whatsoever when it comes to separate vacations. The problem is what you say when you come home from one. If you are honest, you will come sailing in the door and cry out gaily, "Hi! I'm home and I had a wonderful, wonderful time." You will gaily cry that out if you are honest and if you are also not in your right mind. No one in his or her right mind ever has a wonderful time when apart from his or her spouse. No, the proper procedure on returning home from a separate vacation—on which you departed with deep regrets, remember?—is to drag yourself over the stoop with the demeanor of a Bataan Death March survivor.

"Oh, God," I groaned in this case, embracing Xenia, who had arrived an hour earlier, "it's so good to be home!"

"Yes," she said weakly, "especially after I had to spend six hours standing in the Miami airport and the air conditioning had broken down. How was your glee club reunion?"

"Deadly dull," I said decisively, confident that police reports on misdemeanors are not widely distributed. "It rained for three days but I did hear one interesting lecture. It was on seventeenth-century Italianate glee. How was the boat?"

"Sickening. We hit a storm off Tortuga and only fourteen passengers made it to breakfast. Not that the food was worth eating. And the people I had to sit with! I think they were prematurely embalmed. Did you enjoy seeing your old gang?"

"Amazing how they could all grow into such terrible bores. Then I couldn't sleep because of this funny pain in my right elbow and . . ."

I interrupted Barkenthaler at this point to ask how long these competitive tales of woe lasted.

"At least three days," he said. "You see, if each spouse can convince the other that he or she didn't really want to go, had an appallingly bad time as expected, and regretted every single minute of it, then both will get to go on another wonderful, wonderful separate vacation next year."

Glynda never cared much for Barkenthaler and even less after I told her of his advice. "If what you say about Togetherness is true," she wanted to know, "how can so many sweet old couples manage to reach their Golden Anniversaries together?"

The answer, of course, is television. I happen to think that television is the curse of our generation, but I have to admit it has saved countless marriages. I have admitted this ever since reading a survey in *Family Circle* magazine, which found that 78 percent of television watching families engage in "no conversation at all except during commercials." Fortunately, these conversations are generally limited to: "While you're up . . ." or "Did you remember to . . ." or for those given to watching PBS, "Are you awake?"

As for Glynda and me, one of the great challenges our marriage faces is that neither of us cares much for television. "We catch the news and an occasional PBS panel show and that's about all," we say, that being the liberal intellectual thing to say, but that's not true. Glynda dotes on football and I enjoy the cooking demonstrations, having taken up cooking in my later years. Glynda's delighted with my new avocation and praises to the skies any burnt, dried-out, overseasoned *Caneton Roti à l'Alsacienne* I come up with. For when it comes to the culinary arts, she has long since lost any interest that she never had in the first place. Yet she still gamely plays the role of a demon social hostess, throwing her biennial dinner party for six come what may. And I always know how good it's going to be because a week before the guests come, I've already eaten it.

"Now this is the company dinner rehearsal," said Glynda as I approached the table the other evening—a full rehearsal being standard operating procedure before the gala, much-dreaded event. "First, tell me how good the salad is."

"What are we having?" I asked, drawing on all my newfound trendy knowledge. "The usual hot *fromage du chevre* on wilted arugula with raspberry vinegar, pancetta, and a hint of tarragon?"

"No, I'm going to go all-out with the latest gourmet breakthrough, *ancienne cuisine*," she said.

"You mean *nouvelle cuisine*," I told her.

"No, no, taste the salad," she said. "It's tinned, out-of-season fruits in a lime gelatine mold on a bed of fresh iceberg lettuce with a piquant cream dressing."

"Interesting," I said after taking a hesitant bite. "What do you call the piquant cream dressing?"

"Miracle Whip," she said.

I was beginning to get the idea. "And the entree," I said. "I trust you won't be trying mesquite-grilled monk fish with puréed red-and-green pepper sauce. You may recall that when I attempted it last month, repairing the smoke damage cost us $247."

"Mesquite grilling is not part of *ancienne cuisine*," said Glynda. "Taste this interesting casserole instead. I whipped it up from a stock of Campbell's Cream of Mushroom soup into which I carefully introduced an ample portion of Chicken-of-the-Sea. You will note that I gently poured it over Golden Grain egg noodles before garnishing it with fresh, crisp Granny Goose potato chips, none of them broken."

"Incredible!" I said. "Is there a name for it?"

"Tuna Surprise," she said. "What do you think of the string beans?"

"A taste treat," I said. "How did you do them?"

"In my Veg-a-Matic," she said. "I look on it as my *ancienne Cuisinart*. I suppose you expect to get a pomegranate sorbet in an almond cookie tulip cup with a sprig of mint for dessert?"

"No," I said, "tapioca pudding." And, by golly, I was right!

When we had finished, Glynda asked my expert opinion. "Very nostalgic," I said. "All we need are some s'mores."

"I'm only trying to save the world," she said somewhat defensively. *"Ancienne cuisine,* which I invented, is a return to the more innocent times of the fifties, when teenage rebellion was a speeding ticket and Jane Russell's half-draped bosom a national issue."

"Those were the days," I agreed.

"Ancienne cuisine is an attempt to escape the decadence and egocentricity of the current me-oriented gourmet mania," she went on, her chin high. "I would hope in some small way to turn people's attention from their automatic pasta makers back to the problems of the society around them and thereby help make our nation a better place in which to live."

"Boy," I said, "you really hate to cook."

Glynda nodded. "Yes," she said. "That's also true."

So much for food. As for the paucity of our television viewing, we have made brave attempts to remedy the situation. The other day, for example, Glynda was contemplating a bowl of boiled rice. She had been saving it for a week, and it now looked as though she would have to throw it out to make room for a cup of carrots. "Sometimes," she said thoughtfully, "I'm sorry we ever bought that Betamax."

As usual, Glynda had hit the nail on the head. Owning

a video tape recorder is like owning a refrigerator crammed with leftovers. Let me explain: That very same evening, I suggested we curl up romantically after dinner and watch a John Wayne movie I had recorded a week earlier. "Fine," said Glynda, looking up from the television log, "but that means we can't tape a three-star mystery on Channel Two."

Now there's a constant bind. There seems to be something we want to record virtually every evening. This means we can't watch something we've already recorded as you can't record and watch at the same time. It happens I like John Wayne and Glynda likes mysteries. So, after some discussion, we compromised and taped the mystery and spent the evening reading instead. "After all," said Glynda, "then we'll have both."

That made sense. But where were we going to put the mystery? We've accumulated five videotapes. Unfortunately, each already had an old movie preserved on it. So we'd have to erase one old movie to make room for the new old movie. Which one? We finally decided on a tape labeled, "Walt. Mat.," primarily because I couldn't remember what on earth a Walt. Mat. was. Click. Hum. Farewell forever, Walt. Mat.

"Do you think that could have been that Walter Matthau comedy you were so anxious to see?" Glynda said as we were climbing into bed.

"Oh, my God!" I agreed.

Technically perceptive readers might well ask why we simply didn't watch the three-star mystery live and have done with it. The answer, of course, is the fast-forward button. On the rare occasion when we overcome our greed to accumulate still another old movie and instead watch one we have already recorded, this little button makes the entire inane system seem almost worthwhile. What you do with the fast-forward button, needless to say, is zap the commercials. After a lifetime of being subjected to commercials, zapping the purveyors of soaps, cars, and sundries rewards you with glowing feelings of power and revenge. "Take that!" I cry, punching the button that forces these sincerity-exuding figures to scuttle this way and that, babbling incomprehensibly. "Ai-yee! Hah!"

Not only does zapping do wonders for my machismo, it saves time. Thanks to judicious button punching, Glynda and I watched an entire three-hour recorded segment of *Winds of War* in only two hours and twelve minutes. And I figure we could have shaved off at least another hour if Glynda had let me zap Ali McGraw, too.

All in all, however, the problem of recording and watching simultaneously means the four hundred dollars we laid out for the Betamax has done little to solve our problems. What we obviously need, I've explained to Glynda, are two Betamaxes, one to record on while we view a tape on the other. Glynda, in her wisdom, says that we need two Betamaxes exactly as much as we need two refrigerators.

Bereft, for the most part, of television viewing we are thrown on our own avocations. Mine is reading; Glynda's is talking. Make no mistake. Glynda is no brainless yapper. Her conversation is witty, intelligent, urbane, and informative. So are my books. Now, as any perceptive reader will have determined long ago, I am a very easy man to live with—good-natured, tolerant of others' idiosyncrasies, and always willing to compromise generously. Being willing to compromise generously, I long ago suggested that Glynda and I each do what we enjoyed most: She could talk; I could read. This generated an argument which I won hands down: She said how could she talk if I didn't listen? I said that was as simple as falling off a log; after all, I had no difficulty whatsoever reading while she didn't watch me. As usual, while I won the argument, I lost the war. And yet, in one of those incredibly complex methods of generation that are the heart of any marriage, a compromise of the compromise eventually worked itself out: Glynda talked while I read *and* listened.

It wasn't easy. She would come in after dinner, settle herself in her chair, pick up her newspaper, look at me over her reading glasses, and say, "I think I may sell the Haskins's house to the Bodings."

In addition to being a perfect wife, mother, and the inventor of *ancienne cuisine,* Glynda is a demon real estate salesperson, and I always generously encourage her to make as much money as possible. So I put my finger on my place to show that I plan to come back to it soon and say, "That's wonderful! Have they made an offer?"

"No," says Glynda, "I haven't shown it to them yet. But I think it's them to a T."

"Good work," I say and return to my book, girding my mental processes for a session of reading *and* listening. What I listen to, of course, is the tone of her voice. For example, if she now says, "I really think they're going to like it," what I hear is "Da-deedee-da-da-dada-da-di-di." As the tone falls on the very last syllable, this is obviously a statement of opinion. Any husband knows automatically how to respond to a statement of opinion: "I'll bet you're absolutely right!"

She may follow this with: "Of course, it's *full* of dry rot. . . ." Or, as my ear translates that: "Dada-da-*dah*-da-dada. . . ." With the emphasis in the middle and the remark tapering off hesitantly, there's clearly a problem. What's a husband for if not to stand by his wife in her hour of need? "I'm sure you can solve that," I say.

We now get into all the other things that could go wrong with the deal, such as the criminal mind of the selling agent: "Would you believe it? He actually *lied* to me!" Or: "Da-da-dada-da? Da-dadada-*da*-da-da!" Incredulity followed by emphatic anger. We know how to deal with that: "No!" say I with equal incredulity.

In my heart of hearts, I'm convinced that Glynda is at least subconsciously aware of what I am doing and doesn't mind as long as I keep up the semblance of conversational Togetherness. In confirmation of this theory, she will sometimes instruct me to listen if she feels the subject is of grave enough import. "Are you *really* listening?" she'll say. And, in keeping with the unwritten rules of the game, I'll *really* listen. Usually I'll wish I hadn't, as her next remark will be something like "Mordred wants $200 for bongo lessons."

But that's fair. What I think is unfair is when Glynda, in one of her rare, testy moods, traps me. "Da-dada-da-da-dada-da-da," she'll say sweetly.

"That's nice," I'll respond, as this sounds like an innocuous comment on her part.

"What did I say?" she'll suddenly demand with all the glee of a cat pouncing on a wounded butterfly.

Panic! But, oddly enough, when I search back, a word or two of her sentence will be hanging magically in midair. I gratefully scoop them up and clasp them to my bosom. The words are "Botsleys" and "picnic." Phew! "You said," I reply with dignity, "that the Botsleys can come to the picnic."

"I said the Botsleys *can't* come to the picnic," cries Glynda, more triumphant than angry. "And you said that was nice. I knew you never really liked the Botsleys, just because she said you drank too much. . . ." This gets us into a discussion of the Botsleys' merits to which I better damn well listen and I do.

This brings us around to the subject of marital arguments, which I have been avoiding. Many newlyweds enter into connubial bliss under the impression that fighting is good for their marriage. "Are you repressing normal conflicts?" asks the *Ladies Home Journal* in one of those questions the *Ladies Home Journal* dearly loves to ask. "Are you ignoring the seeds of future trouble?" And if you don't put that magazine down, stand up, and belt your loved one on the choppers right then and there, you have the uneasy feeling that you don't give a fig for your marriage.

But picking a fight is not all that easy. The first thing you must do is carefully choose the *size* of the topic to fight about. It should be the most trivial available. For the cardinal rule in marital warfare is: *The bigger the issue, the smaller the fight.* For example, should you say to your spouse, "I beg to differ, I feel that a federal deficit of two trillion dollars is perhaps a shade excessive," the fight will be polite, even-tempered, concluded in five minutes, and about as satisfying as a kamikaze attack on a bowl of cold mashed potatoes. But—ah!—take an opening like, "Just out of curiosity, why did you happen to lead the two of clubs?" This can, as the days pass, expand to embrace intelligence quotients, cooking ability, financial acumen, annoying sexual idiosyncrasies, who takes out the garbage, and ancestors even unto the third generation.

Once you get the hang of it, there's no reason that you, too, can't enjoy cementing the bonds of matrimony with good, knock-down, drag-out fights. But remember that it takes hard work to keep a marriage going. You can't expect simply to sit there and let your partner start all the battles. So, if you've simply been sitting there, start one yourself. A sure-fire starter is: "Why are you so grumpy?" Be ready to follow this up at the first opportunity, which won't be long in coming, with, "Don't shout!" This always adds fuel to the flames. With practice, you can progress to that ideal relationship where you can have a whing-ding go-around over no issue at all. Handy phrases here include: "Don't behave like a child," "Stop nagging," and "I've been meaning to talk to you about your breath."

This is all probably exceptionally good advice, but I fear it is based entirely on hearsay. For my dear wife, Glynda, and I never fight. There are a number of reasons for this, but the primary one is that I am far too much of a gentleman to fight with a lady. Should Glynda in an unthinking moment suggest that I may have had a wee touch too much at the Fays' dinner dansant simply because I came home without my trousers, I rise above it. I may go so far as to say, "I'm sure I don't recall," but after that I will maintain a cool silence to indicate that my thoughts are on far more important matters than the whereabouts of my silly trousers, a subject only a feather-brained woman would find of any interest whatsoever.

Indeed, so gentlemanly am I that I have been known to maintain a cool silence for four days and three nights running. Some envious individuals have actually referred to this incredibly forebearing demeanor of mine as "sulking." Such is the spite of little minds. In the early days of our marriage, Glynda would continue to growl lustily over the current bone of contention even after I had disdainfully brushed it aside with my foot. But she soon saw the folly of that and now, on those rare occasions when we don't see quite eye to eye, her chilly tolerance for my unacceptable point of view almost matches mine.

Another reason we don't fight is that I nobly take the blame. Nay, I don't take the blame; I eagerly seek it out and seize it at every opportunity, flaunting it like a flag. The reason for this is that dear Glynda almost never gets mad at me for what I do. Let me break her favorite pinking shears while attempting to open a paint can and my worst punishment is a bemused smile accompanied by a gentle shake of the head. No, the only time Glynda gets mad at me is when *she* does something wrong. Take the second time she burned the carrots. I attempted to console her as she stared gloomily at the blackened pan. "It could happen to anyone," I said, though I couldn't quite see how.

"It's all your fault," she said.

"It is?"

"Remember last year when the Hathaways came to dinner and I burned a potful then? You promised you'd always remind me to watch the carrots so it wouldn't happen again."

"I don't remember that."

"I was standing right here wearing my plaid skirt and that pink angora sweater you always say makes me look like a rabbit. You had a flyswatter in your right hand, and you said . . . Oh, I remember your exact words! You said. . . ."

How can you argue with that? I don't even remember the Hathaways, much less dinner. If one spouse can remember something, particularly in great detail, it must have happened. And if the other spouse can't remember it, all that indicates is the onset of senility which we don't care to discuss anyway. So I seized the bull by the horns and, in the years that followed, cheerily took the blame for failing to fix a waffle iron I didn't know was broken, allowing Glynda to purchase a car that was really much too large for the garage, not vetoing the puce and salmon wallpaper in the powder room, and not reminding her to leave her glasses on their chain and not to leave the chain God-knows-where she left it.

This course is not only warm, generous, and noble, it frustrates the opposition. Take burned carrots. By now, I must have taken the blame for a good half a ton of burned carrots. Let the faintest whiff of burned carrots waft into the living room and I'm out of my chair in a bound. "Good Lord!" I cry, "I forgot to remind you not to burn the carrots!"

But the frustration builds. In her heart, Glynda knows who burns the carrots. And nothing cloys faster than warmth, generosity, and nobility. "If there's one thing I can't stand," she muttered as she emerged from the kitchen the other evening with the familiar blackened pan in hand, "it's your guiltier-than-thou attitude."

A-hah! A direct assault on my warmth, generosity, and nobility. How could she stoop so low? Back to the old chilly forebearance. I have hopes of setting a record by a week from next Tuesday.

So we don't fight. And I therefore feel far more qualified to offer advice on how to avoid fights. Indeed, I find it hard to believe that any married couple who doesn't want to fight could possibly fight. If there's one thing marriage offers, it's myriad opportunities to avoid fights. Here again the subject of discussion is all-important. I'm convinced that nine out of ten marital arguments are partially caused by one party choosing the wrong topic to discuss. An obvious example would be a wife who chose to chat about the meaning of life at the breakfast table following a loud party at which her husband has made an utter fool of himself and I am not talking about the Fays' dinner dansant. If she wished to avoid a fight (and that might be debatable under such circumstances), she would be far wiser to select a subject of more general interest as the poor soul wobbles up to the table, guilt and an ice bag heaped on his head. "Do you think we should make every effort to increase trade ties with the Peoples' Republic of China?" she might well ask. He could then mumble, "Yes," "No," or "Who gives a damn?" and pick up his paper. No harm done.

We see, then, that one secret to avoiding spats is to pick a topic in which neither side is emotionally involved. Many topics of general interest fairly leap to mind: the three-toed sloth, club soda, the Battle of Thermopylae, the name of those people you met at the beach last summer, quasars, and many, many more. Unfortunately, subjects of general interest are notoriously unstable.

"Did you buy any club soda?" accusingly inquires the aforementioned husband, holding his head together gingerly.

"We wouldn't be constantly running out," says the wife defensively, "if you didn't drink so much."

"If I weren't married to you . . . ," he says, and before you know it, they have progressed from a bottle of club soda to the meaning of life and the grounds for a trial separation.

So the question arises as to how to keep a general subject general. After considerable thought, I have concluded that the problem is more complex than it seems at first glance. Marital arguments are not caused simply by one spouse picking the wrong topic to discuss: *marital arguments are caused when both spouses pick the same wrong topic to discuss at the very same time.* The solution, then, is as plain as the nose on your face: Spouses should avoid at all costs talking about the same subject in the same room at the same time. An ideal marital conversation might go:

"Did you buy any club soda?"

"The three-toed sloth feeds almost exclusively on cecropia."

"I'm sorry Leonidas lost the Battle of Thermopylae."

"Herb and Kitty Forbes!"

"Quasars were first observed. . . ."

I thought so much of this concept that I put it to Glynda for her treasured opinion. She gave me a look. "That's the most ridiculous idea I ever heard of," she said.

I certainly wasn't going to take that lying down. I looked her right in the eye. "I'm sorry Leonidas lost the Battle of Thermopylae," I said.

There are, of course, myriad other ways to avoid a fight. I, personally, have always admired the Dole Response, named in honor of Senator Robert Dole, who first burst forth on the national scene back in 1976 by running for vice president of the United States, he apparently not having much else to do. The good senator was campaigning in Spartanburg, South Carolina, that September when a local reporter asked him if he favored black majority rule for the Union of South Africa.

"Glad you dropped in," said Senator Dole.

Now there's a perfect reply to a stimulating question. It's warm. It's friendly. It makes people feel welcome. The Dole Response is a superb example of efficient interpersonal relations. Unfortunately, Senator Dole couldn't leave it at that. After a pause he said, "I think it's going to come one of these days." Then he said, "I think so, under certain limitations." Then he said, "I favor it with limitations." Then he said, "But I want to check it first." Then he said, "I don't want to get hit with a bomb." The lesson here is never destroy the goodwill you've built up by explaining perfectly reasonable answers. Any husband knows that.

Take the husband who's late to breakfast after a party (*not* the Fay's dansant) and is in serious trouble simply because he arrived through the front door. "Where have you been all night?" his wife may ask, that being a stimulating question.

"Glad you dropped in," he should say, perhaps tossing in a firm handshake to show that he's all in favor of Togetherness.

"What happened to that tacky blonde trollop with the fat hips you were trying to do a bump and grind duet with?" she might well inquire.

"How are the aphids in your mother's primulas?" is a darned good rebuttal at this crucial point, as this demonstrates his devotion to the familial ties that bind as well as his humanitarian concern for the well-being of all creatures great and small.

"Did I see you drive off with her after the party?"

This is a difficult question as any husband will tell you. Probably the best answer here is: "I think we can safely look forward to a steadily improving economy with lower unemployment and diminishing inflation as long as stability can be maintained in the Middle East." This indicates the respondent is no fly-by-night husband but a solid, dependable citizen with an eye to the future and one who is concerned about providing for his loved ones.

All this should surely satisfy any reasonable wife, particularly if the husband can manage to maintain such a high level of dignified replies through two cups of coffee, a shave, and a shirt change before kissing his beloved mate jauntily on the cheek, tipping his hat, and sailing out the door to the office. But woe betide him if he attempts to elaborate on the Dole Response:

"Where have you been all night?"

"Glad you dropped in. Actually, the car wouldn't start. I think the battery was dead. Or maybe it was out of gas. Yes, that's it, it was out of gas. At least it *seemed* to be out of gas. Even though you filled it yesterday afternoon. I guess somebody stole the gas. Or maybe the battery. Or perhaps the left front tire? Or what could have happened was that. . . ."

You probably think I made all this up.

Glad you dropped in.

CHAPTER SEVEN

The Point System

I OFTEN WISH the word hadn't been spread about that I have a black belt in the marital arts. Strangers keep stopping me on the street to plead, "Tell us, O Master, what is the secret of a happy marriage?"

"Decisions," I reply firmly. "Every day every married couple must face myriads of decisions. And the secret of a happy marriage is . . ."

"Yes, O Master?"

". . . never, ever, under any circumstances, make one."

At this point, would-be disciples turn away with testy scowls. How can I hope that these novices could instantly understand the central mystery of the marital arts? After all, it took my dear wife, Glynda, and me years and years to grasp it.

How well I recall that first decision we made together in our innocent youth: where to go on our honeymoon. Glynda had her heart set on a backpacking trip in the Yukon. But I, romantic that I am, insisted on a week's cruise in tropical waters aboard the *SS Moonlight Nights*. I will pass quickly over the two acts of barratry, the incipient mutiny, the drunken kamikaze attack by disgruntled tourist-class passengers on the first-class smorgasbord, and get right down to what Glynda said to me when some malcontent opened the seacocks as the *SS Moonlight Nights* lay at anchor in the muddy harbor of Cocanos. What Glynda said to me was "Your ship is sinking."

That led to the purchase of her car. It was to be our car, but I wanted a sprightly sports coupe and she was expecting at the time. What she was expecting was a four-door, lemon-yellow station wagon. I was delighted to let her have it, particularly when, forty-seven miles past its warranty, it began living up to its color. "Your car," I said happily, "sounds like a threshing machine."

And so it was that we acquired my dry rot. It was no use protesting that I hadn't intended to purchase any dry rot when I said, after looking at forty-two houses: "Oh, heck, I like that little cottage at 132 Upper Terrace." Forever after, it was my little cottage, my dry rot, and my incipient ulcer, this last brought on by worry that one more heavy rainstorm would require us to change our address to 132 Lower Terrace.

Thus it went. But we were learning. Oh, occasionally we would slip, like the time I said I thought our daughter, Malphasia, was old enough to wear lipstick to her junior prom and my daughter, Malphasia, didn't get home until 6:30 A.M. What we were learning was advanced decision-avoidance techniques. For example, we learned never to say "Let's go to the movies." What we said instead was "Would you like to go to the movies?"—thereby putting the decision squarely on the other's shoulders. The proper response, of course, is "Whatever *you* would like." When both parties have said, "Only if *you* would like to" several times, the dread moment has come to decide which movie to go to. Keep in mind here that if either spouse hints what movie he or she prefers, it is henceforth his or her movie for which he or she is totally responsible, God help him or her. Early on, I would foolishly make such bold statements as "Well, *Cinema Today* says that *Crushed Fennel* 'exudes sensitivity' " in hopes that *Crushed Fennel* would thereby become *Cinema Today's* movie and not mine—false hopes, as it turned out. And Glynda once suggested in desperation that we flip a coin to determine whether to see *Vagaries Lost.* Needless to say, *Vagaries Lost* became her flipping movie.

Please don't get the impression, however, that Glynda and I would ever directly criticize the other's decision once it was pinned on the decision maker. We are both far too experienced in the marital arts for that. What we say instead is:

"Gosh, I thought a Czech musical comedy about a boy's dipping sheep in Hradpomuk would be delightful, too."

Or, in the case of restaurants: "Who cares what it cost or how it tasted? Being served by waiters on roller skates was a new experience."

Or, when it comes to vacations: "Gee, your idea of having the whole family get together for a week in a one-bathroom cabin sounded like fun to me. And it's certainly not your fault that we all got that dreadful bug."

We are, in a word, forgiving. And it's certainly not our fault that, in such circumstances, being forgiving is virtually unforgivable.

So if our marriage suffers from a lack of anything, it suffers from a lack of tyranny. How happy Glynda would be if I were an opinionated despot. Think of the points she would accumulate if I were to force my will on her and express whatever rash judgment came to mind. I might be right nine times out of ten. So what? You don't accumulate points in marriage by being right; you lose them by being wrong. So despotism is out. I am too much of a coward to be anything but gentle, kindly, and gallant. Should Glynda ask me how I like her hair, I don't say I like her hair, I say I love her hair, for I've long since found that a woman feels only as good as she thinks her hair looks. But loving a woman's hair is never the end of it:

"Thank you," she says, "but do you like this strand better curled under?"

"That looks nice."

"Or is it less awful if I pull it forward like this?"

"That looks nice."

"Oh, you're no help. Tell me what you really think."

"I think you look beautiful no matter how you fix your hair."

"There, I knew it! You think it looks awful, too."

Ah, well, even we masters of the marital arts are forced

sometimes to express opinions, make decisions, and thereby lose points. In the final analysis, my marriage to Glynda endures not so much because of my skill in Machiavellian maneuvering but because it is based upon the abiding rock of faith. I have faith in a just and benevolent Deity who will unquestionably reward us for our travails here on earth. In other respects, my concept of Heaven is admittedly a bit cloudy, but I envision my entrance into that hallowed spot with incredible clarity. It begins as Glynda and I reach the top of The Golden Staircase. Celestial music swells. The clouds part. Stepping forward to welcome us is that omnipotent old gentleman, Saint Peter, in his white beard and flowing robes. He takes Glynda's hands in his, shakes his head sadly, and in a gentle voice utters those words I have been waiting a lifetime to hear:

"I'm so sorry, my dear," he says, "but you were wrong."

Glynda is naturally puzzled. "Wrong about what?" she asks.

Saint Peter opens his giant Golden Ledger and commences reading from a lengthy list. "For starters," he says, "two spades over one diamond is, too, forcing to game; some cats do, too, like to have their tails pulled; and there is nothing at all kinky about being unable to sleep with the closet door open."

"Oh," says Glynda, slightly crestfallen.

"You might also like to know," says Saint Peter, "that if you had taken Miller Avenue to the airport, as you suggested, instead of Brandon Boulevard, you would have hit an even worse traffic jam and missed not only the 9:15

flight to Chicago but the 11:45 as well. It is also an indisputable scientific fact that men who ask directions from total strangers are sexually inadequate."

"I didn't know that," says Glynda, blushing.

"You probably also didn't know that many responsible husbands over the years have used antique nutcrackers for hammers and yours would have broken anyway on the very next walnut. Moreover, it was quite acceptable to say, 'The damned plants are taking over the house!' when the Swedish Ivy was fortunately smashed. For if it had continued to be overwatered on that rotting sill, the window would have fallen out in the big storm of that December 19, thereby fatally injuring N. M. (Bud) Throckman, who was innocently delivering the laundry."

"I . . . I had no idea."

"Of course not. You probably also never realized that no gentleman could possibly have refused Elsa Mae Purnby's invitation to cha-cha even though he honestly thought her to be an overweight bore. And as for the R.S.V.P. to your cousin Ernest's wedding, it was, indeed, deposited in the mailbox—only to be blown out of the bag of Postman Edward G. Dollan at 14th Avenue and Lincoln the following morning while he was fleeing a Doberman pinscher."

"I should have been more trusting."

"Yes, you should have. You should also have seen that piano lessons for Mordred and Malphasia were a waste of money, that their bad handwriting was due to your genes, and that if you had done your own hair at home, they could have gone to Harvard rather than the community college. You should have further understood that only a saint would have never mentioned that fact."

"I . . . I tried to be a good mother."

"Of course you did. But when Mordred scratched the left front fender, it was extremely fortunate that his father spoke to him sternly (he did *not* shout). For otherwise, Mordred would have embarked on a career of crime culminating in his arrest and conviction for the stickup of the First National Bank on September 22, 1994."

"Oh, to think I've been wrong every single time all these years!" cries Glynda contritely, turning to me with tears in her eyes. "I'm so terribly, terribly sorry."

At that point, I take her in my arms, generously forgive her, and we live happily throughout eternity.

I will concede that there is an extremely remote possibility that the divine arbitrator will find that Glynda was right in these matters and not I. When I envision this contingency, however, I know exactly where I will then be. And it sure won't be Heaven.

THE FAMILY

All God's chillun are brothers and sisters and they sure do fight like it

— The author, in a festive moment circa 1962

CHAPTER EIGHT

Family Planning

THE AMERICAN FAMILY is built on hope and sustained by faith. That enduring hope and faith is perhaps best captured by the following story, which may possibly be apocryphal:

It was a typical PBS panel show. The issue: "When Does Life Begin?" The participants were a serious Catholic priest in clerical garb and rimless glasses; a hearty Episcopalian minister, who was wearing a tweed sports jacket over his black shirt and white collar; and an elderly Jewish rabbi with a wisp of a beard.

The Catholic priest ably defended the Church's position that life begins at the moment of conception. The Episcopalian minister said he refused to confer the rights of the United States Constitution on a fertilized egg. He leaned, he said, toward the moment of birth as the starting point for human life but would settle for the beginning of the second trimester in the interest of harmony.

The camera swung to the rabbi, who was stroking his beard and nodding thoughtfully. "Life begins," said the rabbi slowly, "when the children leave home and the dog dies."

That gets us around to one of the most burning issues of the day: family planning. In the heat of the controversy, all combatants have overlooked the one salient problem of family planning: There is no way to plan a family. Since the dawn of time, billions upon billions of innocent people have been stuck with the families into which they were born through no fault whatsoever of their own. About the only family planning in which they were able to engage was planning how to avoid their families as much as possible.

One of the major spurs to family avoidance planning is Christmas. Planning Christmas itself is of no use whatsoever. Here is a typical Christmas plan for what it's worth—and we all know what it's worth:

6:50 A.M.—Children start jumping up and down. "It's eight o'clock," they lie. "Can we open our presents now?" Daddy suggests that everybody shut up. But Mommy says after all it's Christmas, as though Daddy didn't know that.

6:51 to 9:51 A.M.—Children tear into presents with wild abandon yet manage somehow to keep meticulous track of precisely how many presents each of the other children is getting. Thanks to Mommy, everyone gets exactly the same number which cost exactly the same amount of money. Daddy does his utmost to burn the gaily colored wrapping paper as fast as the children fling it away. He burns not only the wrapping paper but the ribbons, the credit slips, and the instructions on how to insert Tab A into Slot 1467(b). For excitement, he also starts a chimney fire.

9:52 A.M.—Mommy opens her present from Daddy. This being an odd-numbered year, it's a blouse. (On even-numbered years, it's a sweater.) Mommy tells Daddy her surprise was just what she wanted.

9:53 A.M.—Daddy opens his present from Mommy. It is a wristwatch home entertainment center, containing a tiny television set, a stereo cassette player, a barometer, and six video games. Daddy tells Mommy it's just what he wanted even though it doesn't tell time. It doesn't work, either.

10:00 A.M.—Daddy turns on the Salad Bowl to watch the fighting Grambling Tech Antelopes (3–6–1) play the Tri-State Normal Coyotes (4–7) in the holiday pigskin classic. The children rush outside to break their presents.

12:57 P.M.—The score is tied 42–42. The Antelopes are about to attempt a field goal with twelve seconds left. The doorbell rings. It is Uncle Uriah, Aunt Bellephone, Grandfather Gringe, and assorted little cousins, most of them wet.

1:03 P.M.—"Would anyone like a cocktail before dinner?" asks Daddy. Mommy says it is three hours before dinner, as though Daddy didn't know that.

1:04 to 4:17 P.M.—Daddy, Uncle Uriah, and Grandfather Gringe argue politics, religion, economics, and whether Daddy put too much vermouth in the martinis. They finally agree on something: They agree Daddy should keep experimenting until he gets it right.

4:18 P.M.—Mommy calls everyone to dinner. Aunt Bellephone says it is the best canned jellied cranberry sauce she has ever tasted in her life, although she prefers her own homemade whole-berry kind herself. The children break bread together, the better to throw it.

6:07 P.M.—Grandfather Gringe falls asleep in the candied yams. Uncle Uriah says he guesses it's time they took him home. Daddy doesn't argue with that one, either.

9:57 P.M.—The last child has been put to bed, the last dish washed. Mommy admits to jangled nerves and a splitting headache. She says bravely that it was all worth it, though, because Christmas comes but once a year. As though Daddy didn't know that.

It's soul-trying times like these that lead men to desperate measures. My friend Henry Narsen has gone so far as to file for divorce. He does not, God forbid, want to divorce his wife, Calomel, whom he loves dearly. He wants to divorce an uncle, three aunts, two first cousins, and his brother-in-law. As this constitutes his entire family, with the exception of Calomel and one daughter, his antipathy toward his relatives would at first glance appear unusual.

"Look," he says, "my relatives aren't so bad as relatives go, and I can never wait until they do. The fact is that we've got nothing much in common and there's no reason to expect that we should. If I met them at a party, I'd never invite a single one of them to dinner. So, how come I've got to eat with them half a dozen times a year? Of course, we get along fine as long as we avoid such topics as politics, religion, current events, sex, sports, movies, books, food, prices, children, each other, or the weather."

As an expert on the subject, I agreed that family gatherings could be exasperating, but surely he didn't have grounds for divorce. "Grounds!" he cried. "In addition to incompatibility, I'm suing Aunt Winifred for aggravated guilt tripping. I had a champagne cocktail or three at her daughter Earleen's wedding and decided it would be a fun idea to go skinny dipping in the fish pond. So every week in the mail I get a pamphlet from Aunt Winifred extolling the virtues of the Serene Sunset Home for Problem Drinkers."

"Sounds rather thoughtful of her," I said.

"As I told her the last time we spoke," said Henry with dignity, "if there's one problem I don't have, it's a problem drinking."

Henry's maiden Aunt Griselda has been served for parenting without a license. "She keeps telling our daughter, Anastasia, that if she has intimate relations with a man before marriage, the boogeyman will get her."

"How old is Anastasia now?" I asked.

"Thirty-two," said Henry. "Then there's my brother-in-law, Bud. Talk about sartorial embarrassment! Whenever we go out for dinner, he wears white leather loafers, double-knit polyester pants, and an aloha shirt. Then when the headwaiter gives him a tie, he complains that it doesn't match. I would've left him long ago if he hadn't loaned me ten grand."

"Now that's what relatives are for," I said.

"At five points over prime?" said Henry.

I had to admit that relatives could sometimes be aggravating, interfering, embarrassing, and boring. "But if you divorce all of them, Henry," I asked, "where will you spend Thanksgiving and Christmas?"

"In a cafeteria," he said. "When it comes to striking up an interesting conversation with the person next to me, I'll go with the odds."

So the nuclear family is exploding. Most sociologists blame this phenomenon on the Sexual Revolution, the Generation Gap, or the threat of Soviet aggression in Western Europe. I blame television. I back up this contention with the results of a survey which asked children between four and six years old which they preferred, television or daddy. A total of 44 percent replied, "Television." My friend Eustace Pankin was as shocked by this figure as I. I was shocked that it was so high; he, after pursuing some personal research on the subject, was shocked that it was so low. But let him tell his story in his own words (as though you could stop him):

When I heard that disturbing news (begins Eustace in his own words), I came straight home and put the question to my five-year-old son, Adelbard, who has a keen analytical mind for one so young. "Adelbard," I said, "which do you prefer . . ."

"Shhh, Daddy," he said, "the commercial's over."

I glanced at our nineteen-inch solid-state Pentasonic TV with Kolor-Hold. The kid was right as usual. "Hollywood Bowling for Dollars" was back on the air. But I was laying for him at the next commercial. "Okay, Adelbard," I said grimly, "which do you prefer, television or Daddy?"

"Well, Daddy," he said thoughtfully, "like any normal, red-blooded American kid, I spend one-third of my waking time in the living room watching something. And frankly, I would rather watch tv than you."

"I can understand that tv is more animated, colorful, and visually pleasing, Adelbard," I said, "and I admire your analytical skills in ferreting out that fact. But where can you turn for information? Who cheers you up when you're blue?"

Adelbard nodded. "Yeah, it also does that."

"You're forgetting," I said, "that every boy needs a pal who'll play games with him when he's bored."

"You bet, Daddy," he said. "And there's nothing like sitting here with a joy stick in my hand, blasting Commie Alien Pree-Verts from Outer Space off the tube."

"Shhh," said the woman on my left. It was my wife, Mary Jane, or perhaps Sue. "The 'I Love Lucy' rerun is on."

At the first commercial I turned to her. "Mary Jane," I said . . .

"Sue," she said.

"Sue," I said, "do you realize Adelbard prefers tv to me, his own father?"

"Adelbard who?" she said. "Oh, I love this scene where Ricardo brings Lucy the bouquet of violets with the bee in it. There's something so traditional and enduring about reruns, isn't there?"

It wasn't a half-hour later that the phone rang. And

119 ———

rang. And rang. "Oh, that reminds me," said Sue absently, "did I tell you your mother was in the hospital, having been struck a glancing blow by a falling grand piano?"

"Don't tell me during 'Monday Night Football,' " I said.

As the evening and Johnny Carson wore on, however, I waxed philosophical. "Sue," I said, "do you think all American families these days are just like ours?"

"I certainly don't," she said hotly. "The Hitcherbees across the street have a twenty-one-inch Pulsar Splendorsonic with Digital Channelizing and Remote-Control Vertical Tuning."

Something snapped. I vowed then and there to take drastic measures to eliminate the horrible situation into which our little family had been trapped. In less than a week, success crowned my desperate efforts! I was able to sell Adelbard to a black-market adoption agency and with the proceeds I purchased a twenty-one-inch Pulsar Splendorsonic with Digital Channelizing and Remote-Control Vertical Tuning. It, Sue (or Mary Jane, as the case may be), and I are now as happy together as any other closeknit American family. Dumb survey! What it should have done is asked daddies which they preferred, television or kids.

But where there is a problem in our society, we can count on the free enterprise system to come up with a solution—sometimes workable, sometimes not. Thus it should come as no surprise that even now a new service is being offered to those in need. It's called "Rent-a-Family," and one of its first customers was a man I know named Eldon Cheevey. An orphaned bachelor at twenty-four, Cheevey was a cautious young man who generally thought things through. After reading a brochure from Rent-a-Family, however, Cheevey leapt at the opportunity.

The plan certainly had its advantages: For a mere $15,000 a year, Cheevey was able to rent the perfect wife. Her name was Dearest. She kept his apartment as neat as a pin, never told him he smoked too much, rubbed his neck without demanding he return the favor, and was totally immune to headaches. When he told her of his daily tribulations at the office with Mr. Klatch (not his real name), she never once responded with, "You wouldn't believe what happened to me today in the Safeway parking lot!" Instead, she merely muttered sympathetically, "Poor dear," and went into the kitchen to turn out another perfect chocolate mousse.

So pleased was Cheevey with his rented wife that he rented a kindly, silver-haired mother named Mom, who didn't care a whit if he failed to call her once a week or even if he forgot her birthday. "Land o' Goshen, son," Mom would say, "you've got a lot more important matters on your mind than worrying about me."

With Mom, at no extra cost, came Dad, a wise, pipe-puffing gentleman in a cardigan with leather elbow patches who was a dead ringer for Walter Cronkite. Dad was a great guy who agreed with everything Cheevey said, thereby proving his wisdom, and who never offered advice unless asked even though his securities portfolio was doing 47.3 percent better than the Dow Jones averages.

Cheevey couldn't make up his mind whether to rent

children or not. But after carefully observing those of his friends, he finally decided that the joys of parenthood outweighed the woes—if you played your cards right. So when the urge came over him to read a bedtime story, he would rent a couple of cuddly tots (both housebroken) for the evening. Every now and then he'd rent a daughter to take to the zoo. And he was the proudest parent in the audience when his strapping rented son ($69.95 for the day, mileage included) graduated first in his class from Skarewe University. What he was proudest of was that he had saved $50,000 on his son's education.

"Just think," he said happily to Dearest one morning, "I have all of the pleasures of a family and none of the drawbacks."

"You're absolutely right, dear," said Dearest, serving him two perfect fried eggs with the whites hard and the yolks runny.

That was the day Mr. Klatch gave him the sack, and he was run over by a pushcart. Instead of a cold martini and a warm "Poor dear" when he arrived home, he found Dearest packing. "Sorry, Mr. Cheevey," she said coldly, "I've found a better paying job as a mother superior in a tuna-packing plant."

He called Mom and Dad, but they regretfully informed him that, due to his unemployed status, their contract was automatically terminated. "Quite frankly, Cheevey," said Dad, "I'm darned glad I won't have to listen to any more of your hare-brained political theories."

Cheevey contemplated suicide. He went down to the depot and asked the attractive information clerk,

Cynthia S., the arrival time of the next train he could throw himself under. Cynthia, a reasonably good woman, saved him from himself for herself. They were married, had three children, and settled down to live happily, now and then, off and on, ever after.

There's a certain forgivable smugness about Cheevey these days. For he thinks he's learned what families are all about. "When you've got a family, you've got troubles," he says with a wry little smile. "But also vice versa."

CHAPTER NINE

Choosing the Right Baby for You

IF IT'S DIFFICULT to plan a family, it's easy to plan your babies. Unfortunately, as the poet Robert Burns so eloquently put it: "The best laid loves o' mice and men gang aft pregnant." But planning babies is certainly worth the old college try, especially these days when a baby is going to cost you a good $100,000 over the next twenty-one years. Consequently, many conservative couples are opting instead for a Rolls Royce Silver Cloud or matching his and hers Ferraris on the grounds that the upkeep is lower, a good car more impresses the neighbors, and unlike most babies, the initial investment can be recovered when it becomes a classic. "Cindi and I talked about having a baby," says Brent C., a Manhattan yuppie, "briefly. But luckily Cindi has a two-year-old nephew and we had the good sense to borrow it for an evening to get a feel for how it was to have a child. We didn't like it." Brent and Cindi, who already owned a Porsche, put their money into municipals, and are quite happy with that blessed event. "Show me a child who pays 9.8 percent tax free," says Brent proudly.

Fortunately for the preservation of the species, however, the human race has never been noted for its rationality, and couples, despite all logic, go on having babies. At least they did up until now. But I fear that the scientific community, which brought us fluorocarbons, the hydrogen bomb, and daytime television, may finally have gone too far. Some Japanese researchers have now announced that by the year 1990, if not sooner, they will have perfected a chromosome-splitting technique that will enable parents to select the sex of their unborn children, God help us all. Anyone who doesn't promptly realize that this frightening development will doom the institution of marriage as we have all come to know and love it either lacks imagination or has never been married.

Scene: *A living room in the year 1992. Fred Frisbee looks up from his newspaper and notices that his wife, Felicia, is knitting. . . . Could it be? Yes! It's a bootie!*
FRED: Darling! Does this mean . . .
FELICIA (*blushing*): Yes, dear, we will soon hear the pitter-patter of little feet.
FRED: Wonderful! And I already have the name, Fred, Junior.

FELICIA: She'll never get into Wellesley with a name like that.

FRED: She? But you're forgetting we can choose now. Surely we want a boy.

FELICIA: *We* can choose? If I have to spend nine months manufacturing this child, I think the choice should be mine as to what I'm going to manufacture.

FRED: Wait a minute. The decision affects me as much as you. The sex we pick makes a statement about our marriage. Nothing says you these days like your child.

FELICIA: Right. And when you roll our adorable little girl down the street in her carriage, everyone will know what a kind, generous, sweet man you are.

FRED: They'll know who wears the pants in our little family. If you think for one minute that I want to be the laughingstock of the Zenith Point Racketball Club . . .

FELICIA (*sighing*): No wonder the divorce rate has doubled in the past two years. Really, Fred, there's no reason we can't discuss this like two mature adults.

FRED (*calming down*): You're absolutely right, Felicia. Now, speaking dispassionately, tell me why on earth you'd want a girl, seeing that for millennia girl babies have been exposed on hillsides, sold to the highest bidder, isolated in purdah, and otherwise treated as heaven-sent disasters.

FELICIA (*biting her lip*): Kindly don't lay your guilt on me. And please remember that girls are much easier to raise than boys. They're more helpful and cooper-

ative, and they don't go around breaking windows
with rocks.

FRED: That's because they throw like girls. Boys, on
the other hand, are far more manly.

FELICIA: Exactly. And that's why boys are likely to
turn to alcohol, drugs, and crime. Think of the grief
a boy would cause us when he became a teenager.

FRED: By getting pregnant?

FELICIA: At least a girl won't grow up to incinerate civilization. Females hate war. And don't tell me that's
what Margaret Thatcher said when . . .

FRED (*nodding*): . . . when she invaded the Falklands.
What's more, I never would've enjoyed playing
catch with Margaret Thatcher.

FELICIA (*angrily*): Oh, you only want a boy in order to
fill your frustrated athletic expectations.

FRED: And what about you? You want a girl to dress
up and glory over when she has dates and goes to
proms. Talk about identifying!

FELICIA: You and your typical male-conceived sexual
stereotypes!

(*There's a moment of tense silence. Finally Fred's
shoulders relax and now it's he who attempts to save
the marriage.*)

FRED (*taking Felicia's hand*): Look, I've got an idea. Why
don't we do what parents have done for millions of
years: Let the Good Lord decide.

FELICIA: (*thoughtfully*): You may have something there.

FRED (*smiling wryly*): Yes, it's not only that God's wiser
and more experienced than we; it's that He doesn't
have to take the heat. There, isn't that a swell idea?

FELICIA (*angrily snatching away her hand*): What do you
mean, *"He"?*

Ah, the planning that goes into the next generation! It's
no wonder we're such an admirable species. While some
are planning to have fewer babies and some are planning
to have better babies, one of the most envied figures in our
society is constantly planning to have more babies. I am
speaking, of course, of the welfare mother.

You can scarcely go into any private club in the land
these days without encountering some gentleman who is
banging his glass of Jack Daniels on the bar and jealously
extolling the brilliance of welfare mothers for having discovered the secret of the easy life, which, after all is the
goal of The American Dream. "They just go right on
having kids in order to keep increasing their income" is
the way these fans generally express their admiration for
the welfare mother's acumen.

Wishing to see for myself the results of such astuteness, I
was lucky enough to obtain an interview with Mrs.
Miranda MacNeil, one of the most competent welfare
mothers in the country. Mrs. MacNeil, who was recently
named Welfare Mother of the Year, lives with her ten
children in a snug, two-bedroom apartment in a district
known as The Inner City, which is located conveniently to
everywhere. She was kind enough to outline for me the
highlights of her meteoric career:

"I decided to devote my life to welfare motherhood
when I was fifteen," said Mrs. MacNeil, who was wearing a fashionable "bulky look" flour-sack dress which

matched the layettes of the twin infants in her arms. "You have to start young if you want to make a killing in the welfare mother industry—Alan, stop biting your sister— The first thing I did was to move—put that knife down, Mary Alice—to California, where welfare mothers are really respected. I was fortunate enough—Peter, please don't kick Mother in the shins while she's talking—to have four children in three years. A lot of professional welfare mothers might have retired right there to rest— stop wailing, Nancy Jo; you *cannot* keep that rat as a pet— on their laurels, but I was ambitious. I couldn't resist the temptation to have Herbert—he's the one over there with the measles—and the extra $14.92 a week he'd bring in. After that, there was no stopping me—Would you mind holding Philip and Philipina while I change Millicent's diapers?—I suppose I was just carried away with the urge to strike it rich.

"Of course, the rules of the profession don't allow a man to live in the house, so I was forced to sacrifice my marriage for my career. But the rewards—Freddie, you put out that fire in that mattress right this very minute—have made it all worthwhile. So let me take this opportunity to thank all those who have made it possible for me to reach the top in my chosen field, beginning with my husband, George, who was so very understanding. 'Go ahead, Miranda,' he said, when I asked him to move out, 'I won't stand in your way.' He still visits me occasionally, however, and I know I wouldn't be where I am today—you spray Baby Bobby one more time in the eye with that roach killer, Norma Jean, and Mother will be forced to reprimand you severely—without his loving help."

As a top welfare mother, Mrs. MacNeil takes in a whopping $198.00 a week or approximately $1.72 an hour—the maximum a grateful state can bestow. "But it's not just the easy money," she says. "It's the satisfaction of knowing you're the very best at your job."

Asked whether she would do it all over again, Mrs. MacNeil hesitated. "Well, given my druthers," she said thoughtfully, "I think I'd druther be a rattlesnake farmer."

So family planning, one way or another, is now *de rigueur*. Unfortunately, the government appears determined to make it more difficult than ever. I had thought that if the government stepped into the field of family planning, it would license parents. The government dearly loves licensing people to do things. It licenses them to drive cars, fly airplanes, and go fishing. Surely motherhood requires as much, if not more skill than hooking a small-mouth bass. Yet as matters stand, any unskilled, ill-equipped, untrained, accident-prone couple can willy-nilly help shape the next generation without so much as a by-your-leave. No wonder the nation's in a mess. But, no, instead of licensing parents, our lawmakers appear bound and determined to confer the full rights of the United States Constitution on fertilized eggs, all of which would enjoy the blessings of American citizenship as long as they were, needless to say, American. And that's a problem right there. For if children born on American soil of foreign parents are automatically American, surely eggs fertilized on American soil are equally American. And what is to prevent hordes of foreigners from honeymooning in America

131 ———

so that in later life their fertilized eggs can swarm through our immigration barriers? The very thought of America being overrun by alien-looking fertilized eggs would churn the stomach of any patriot.

That's the conservative view. For the liberal view of such legislation. I refer you to Minerva Hibbins, author of *Sex and the Single Egg.* "It's all well and good to provide Constitutional protection to the fertilized egg," says the noted feminist, "but what about the unfertilized egg? Surely she, too, is alive. And surely, if her mother is an American, she, too, is an American. Should she be deprived of her American citizenship simply because she hasn't mated?"

In *Sex and the Single Egg,* Ms. Hibbins outlines the cruel fate awaiting her heroine, Eva the Ovum: Born in the warm depths of the ovarian bower, Eva shyly ventures forth to hide coyly in the soft folds of the fallopian tube, there to await the arrival of her eager swain. Monogamous to the core, she seeks no casual relationships or one-night stands; she will mate only in holy union for life. But what happens to Eva in these barbarous times when she is unprotected by the majesty of the law? Millions of suitors may set forth to woo this precious jewel, only to be fouly murdered—every single one of them—in the attempt, thereby leaving Eva to expire, alone and unfulfilled, her all-too-brief life wasted in cold spinsterhood. Or, worse, poor Eva may become a hapless victim of the Pill, condemned to spend her days imprisoned within the ovarian bower, subject to no habeus corpus proceedings, arbitrarily denied the right to travel—a right enjoyed today even by avowed Communists. Once Americans are aware of Eva's plight, Ms. Hibbins says, there can be no question that their sense of justice will drive them to support vociferously the Equal Rights for Eggs Amendment.

But what, you may well ask, about the swain? We have already seen them perishing in a slaughter unequaled in the annals of human genocide. Does no one speak for them? Rest assured that where there are innocent victims, from the harp seals to the frobish lousewort, tender human hearts will come to their rescue with an organization. Thus was born the Fair Play for Spermatozoa Committee. We members of the Committee are fully aware that hitherto there has been little clamor to provide Constitutional protection for these little fellows. It is all too true that their numbers are legion and their mission virtually impossible. No wonder our society has always held their lives cheap. Yet their dedication, their determination, and their indomitable grit should be held aloft to one and all as Americanism at its finest. We need but to make the nation cognizant of their heart-stirring story.

Consider, then, the apocryphal history of but one of these unborn countrymen of ours. Let us, for the sake of identification, call him Harold. For his first ninety days, tiny Harold lies idly about, growing daily, gathering strength, practicing swimming, and mustering resolve. At last, looking like a cuddly tadpole, he is deemed mature enough for The Quest. His single-minded goal: to seek out, woo, and win Eva the Ovum. No knight vowing to free a princess imprisoned in a tower was ever endowed with more chastity, felicity, and nobleness of purpose. Ta-

133 ——

da! Ta-da! With eighty million or so of his fellows, each equally determined, Harold bravely sets forth on his mission, a mission far more hazardous than faced by the heroes of the Light Brigade. His little tail flailing away, he struggles onward, ever onward. Excelsior! One by one, to the left and right of him, his companions fall by the wayside. At last he and he alone wins through to his soulmate. They are joined as the Good Lord decreed, and with His blessings, they go forth together to the sanctity of the womb where they will flourish and multiply.

Isn't that a beautiful story? *But that's not the way it is.* In these decadent times, this is the way it usually is: No sooner has Harold set forth on his glorious Quest than he and his companions run into an impenetrable elastic barrier. Time and again, they butt their little heads against this unyielding wall with all the force at their command—to no avail. They hurl themselves forward and rebound over and over, knowing no other course, until at last they collapse and expire from sheer frustration. Or, even more poignant, they find their way clear. With hopes high, they dash forward—only to plunge blindly into a sea of noxious, lethal poisons from which there is no escape. Or, most cruel of all, Eva's mother is a feminist on the Pill or a Catholic on the rhythm method. It is then that Harold struggles ever onward, overcoming insuperable odds, triumphantly winning through in the end to the silken fallopian folds, which he eagerly parts—only to discover that no one's home. Is it any wonder that he succumbs to a broken heart?

Some masculinists argue that they have the right to do

what they wish with their own spermatozoa. "Keep your laws off our bodies," they say. But surely an end must be put to this vicious practice of spermatocide. If a fertilized egg can be sheltered by the Constitution, surely these doughty little battlers also deserve the fruits of American citizenship. I have done my best to enlist the support of my dear wife, Glynda, in this crusade to give every spermatozoa a chance. You know what she said? She said, "Go lay an egg."

Well, that gives you some idea of the difficulties you face in trying to plan a family. There is a bright side, however. For scientists, after giving us the Pill, are now hard at work providing us with test tube miracles. Hardly a day goes by without some smashing advance in the fields of *in vitro* fertilization and genetic engineering. That's scientists for you: First they busily figure out ways for us to enjoy the pleasures of sex without the consequences; then they busily figure out ways for us to enjoy the consequences of sex without the pleasures. It just shows you what God could do if He only had the technological know-how.

So the scientists offer us hope. I personally hope that now they have given us embryonic transplants and immaculate petri-dish conceptions, they will turn their attention to the end product. With genetic engineering scoring new breakthroughs daily, there is no reason young couples can't look forward to having babies with long, silky hair, floppy ears, adoring eyes, and enough intelligence to be housebroken by the age of three months. Or, better yet, why can't our geneticists limit the number of apertures? Eyes and ears are fine, but all those others! It is an infant's apertures that break the spirits of even the most devoted parents. Think of the number of times a weary mother must blow the nose of a leaky child before it reaches the age of seven. As for me, I'd rather not think about it at all.

In addition to the aperture problem, babies have a number of other defects, their chief one being that they grow into children. Over the years, I have spent a great deal of time with children, and I have found children to be, generally speaking, childish. After thirty seconds or so, a conversation with anyone under twelve will tend to drag. "How old are you? . . . Is that so? . . . And where do you go to school? . . . My, my. . . . And do you see any parallels between the Russian intervention in Afghanistan and the way we propped up a series of corrupt regimes in Vietnam? . . . No, that's Vietnam. V–i–e–t. . . ."

I know I will be accused of ageism, but children are, on the whole, untidy, self-centered, and intellectually inferior to adults. The average child is simply not as well educated, as knowledgeable, as mentally agile, or as emotionally mature as the average adult. Most of them under the age of four have atrocious table manners and make horrible dinner partners. How many dinner parties would I be invited to if I were given to banging my glass with my spoon, dribbling my mashed potatoes down my chin, and hiding under my chair? Neither are they our equals physically. For example, I loathe playing tennis with opponents aged eight or under as I beat them so easily and they are, for the most part, very poor losers. (I also loathe playing tennis with opponents aged nine or over as they might very well beat me, which I would enjoy even less as children, for the most part, are very poor winners.)

With all this in mind, I find it amazing that so many young people opt for a baby rather than a Rolls Royce Silver Cloud—amazing and deeply heartwarming. It is as though each foresees only the good points of having children, as when they fall trustingly asleep in your arms, bravely swim across a lake to win your approval, or thoughtfully call you on your birthday from a distant land. So, all in all, I'm wholeheartedly for young people having children, particularly my own offspring. For when they have children, they will see what I went through raising them. And then maybe they'll come visit me once a week. Is that so much to ask?

CHAPTER TEN

Raising the Perfect Child

FOR MILLIONS OF years, untrained, unskilled, amateur parents have been raising their children without the faintest idea of how to go about it. All they knew was to yell and scream and occasionally belt them one willy-nilly. Consequently, their children grew up to be parents who yelled and screamed and occasionally belted their offspring when circumstances and frayed nerves demanded. But in recent times all that has begun to change. Now there is a constant stream of articles, books, and even adult education courses on how to raise the perfect child. When I think of this radical departure from the past, I think of my friend Philo Gompers. Philo, the father of an amateur child named Irwin, not only underwent Parent

Effectiveness Training, but he enrolled in a Responsive Parent Improvement Program and joined a study group entitled "Children: The Challenge"—which they certainly are. Like any well-trained parent, Philo exhibited the required amount of delight on bumping into Irwin on the sidewalk outside Irwin's school:

"Good morning, Irwin," said Philo, extending his hand, "and who do you think is going to win the race for alderman? I ask you this as all my instructors agree I must stop treating you as a puppy who needs to be housebroken and start treating you with the respect and courtesy I afford human beings of the adult persuasion."

"Oh," said Irwin, "it's you."

"Let us talk about topics of mutual interest in order to establish and maintain a helping relationship," said Philo. "What are you doing?"

"I'm setting fire to the school," said Irwin.

"I won't ask why because that would invite you to blame others, offer excuses, and dwell on feelings, rather than behavior," said Philo. "Instead, I will merely be prepared to offer my aid if needed."

"Okay," said Irwin. "Got a match?"

"But in a friendly, nonjudgmental way, let me suggest that you evaluate your behavior yourself," said Philo. "Is what you are doing helpful to you?"

"Yeah," said Irwin. "It'll help keep me from flunking today's quiz in Interpersonal Relationships."

"Let me assist you in constructing more responsible behavior," said Philo. "Without my experienced counsel, you may evolve a plan that is overly ambitious. Perhaps you should consider smaller, more realistic goals so you can enjoy success and thereby build the self-confidence you will need in facing life."

"Okay," said Irwin. "I'll just burn down the Interpersonal Relationships classroom."

"Allow me to reward your good thinking with high praise," said Philo. "And should your plan fail, rest assured that I won't punish you as punishment creates isolation and hostility."

"Swell," said Irwin. "Where's the match?"

"First, in order to strengthen your motivation and increase your involvement with me as a parent, I'd like you to make a solemn commitment to your plan," said Philo. "Which would you prefer, a handshake, a verbal agreement, or a written contract?"

"Put her there," said Irwin. "Now do I get the match?"

But the moment of denouement was too much for Philo, and rationality took over. "Absolutely not," he said firmly. "But in treating you as I would any mature, responsible adult, I'll see you get ten to twenty instead for attempted arson. Officers, do your duty!"

Philo still has hopes for Parent Effectiveness Training. "But first," he says, "someone has to train our children not to treat us as puppies being housebroken."

Exactly. We now see that all the articles, books, and adult education courses on the subject are directed toward raising the perfect child for the benefit of the child. What about raising the perfect child for the benefit of the parent? If you want to raise a perfect child from the child's point of view, the obviously correct procedure is to spoil it rotten. I was talking about spoiled children at lunch the other day with Jerome. A nostalgic look softened his eye. "Yes," he said, "I can remember picking up a plate of creamed succotash at a party, pouring it onto the carpet and shouting, 'I *hate* creamed succotash!' "

"When was that?" I asked.

"Last week," he said.

"But, Jerome," I said, "you're thirty-two years old. Why do you want to behave like a spoiled child?"

"I have made a careful study of children," said Jerome, "and I've found that spoiled children invariably get more than their fair share. So I decided to be spoiled."

"Really, Jerome," I said, "that sounds like the height of self-indulgence."

He looked surprised. "Who else would I prefer to indulge?" he said.

I'll have to admit he had whetted my interest. "What happened after you spilled your succotash?" I asked.

"Oh, the hostess, who was a bit flustered, suggested we all go into the living room. Naturally, I folded my arms and shouted, 'No! Capital N, O. No!' "

"Naturally," I said. "But what did that get you?"

"Another helping of pecan pie with whipped cream. I dearly love pecan pie with whipped cream, and it's loaded with calories. I'm trying to put on another fifteen pounds so I'll get even better at pushing."

"Pushing's helpful?"

"I'd never have gotten in to see Robert Redford at the Palace without shoving my way to the head of the ticket line. Lousy seats, though."

"So you stormed out?"

"No, I lay on my stomach in the middle of the aisle, kicked my feet, and screamed bloody murder so no one could hear what was going on."

"And that got you two in the fifth row center?" I asked, reaching for the basket of bread.

"No, in the loges," he said, snatching the basket out of my hands and clutching it to his chest.

"Come on, Jerome," I said. "Learn to share."

But he just shook his head and said, "Mine!"

I sighed. "Whatever happened to common, ordinary politeness in this country?" I mused.

Jerome shrugged. "Where does it get you?" he said.

I wish I'd seen the waiter coming with the succotash. It would have saved me a shoeshine. "Enough of your spoiled ways, Jerome," I said, rising angrily. "I'm leaving. Fork over your half the check."

He smugly folded his arms, looked up at me with a smirk and said, "I don't have to if I don't want to."

That's when I let him have it with the mashed potatoes. I *hate* mashed potatoes. And talk about the rejuvenating effects of self-indulgence! I walked out of that restaurant feeling like a seven-year-old.

But no sane parent wants to live with a spoiled seven-year-old. A spoiled child may be a perfect child from the child's point of view, but not from good old dad's. Good old dad doesn't want some dumb kid who's constantly whining to be taken to some stupid baseball game or some boring circus. The perfect child to dad is the one who causes the least possible trouble.

Needless to say, raising such a perfect child is not as easy as falling off a log. Dads must devote at least several minutes a day to the task. The secret is to start the very moment the child is born. Remember that the perfect child is *always, always, always* breast fed. I know I will be accused of holding this opinion merely because I am a man. That's true. But when Mother says this, tell her all competent studies agree that Mother's milk is far better for Baby than cow's milk, goat's milk, or Dad getting up in the middle of the night. Mother, being a mother, will be forced to go along with this; but watch out for devious stratagems. I recall the week Mordred arrived: After several sleepless nights, dear Glynda claimed that Mordred had been born with teeth. We switched to the bottle. Now I wasn't able to locate Mordred's teeth for a good six months. And I figured if babies were born with teeth, there would have been a lot of sore mothers down through the ages before the invention of the bottle. But as Glynda pointed out, her opinion on the subject was far more painfully arrived at than mine.

Frankly, I'm not sure how today's modern father can escape changing diapers. In my day it was easy: When given the first opportunity, you simply grasped the safety pin and poked it gently into the child's bottom. This caused the child to yelp and the mother to snatch it away from you. From that point on, you were viewed as a bumbling clod and never allowed near a safety pin again. Unfortunately, the safety-pinned diaper has gone the way of the iron maiden, and all the modern father can do is resort to just plain clumsiness. I would suggest fastening the disposable diaper either so loosely that it falls off just when

Dad is bouncing Baby on the newly re-covered couch or so tightly that Baby turns blue. This is, of course, far more difficult than jabbing with a pin, but the results are worth the effort. (Let me say here that acquired clumsiness is a well-rewarded virtue in marriage. By chipping a few plates and spilling a small flood of water on the floor, I have been excused from dish washing for years. Moreover, by giving the subject my most intense concentration, I have never learned to make a bed neatly. "You just can't make a bed neatly," Glynda will say with that oh-you-men! tone of despair wives so often adopt. And what can I do but sadly agree?)

Having disposed of disposable diapers, let us turn to that thrilling moment when Baby takes its first step. What should you do? You should gently kick Baby's legs out from under Baby. Walking leads to a Pandora's Box of troubles and should be vigorously discouraged until Baby is mature enough to obey simple commands. Once Baby can walk at the reasonable age of three or four, the very first thing you should teach it is to heel. Show me a baby who can heel and I'll show you a perfect child. There you are in the department store and Baby toddles off toward the display of Christmas tree ornaments. "Heel, Baby!" you shout and Baby immediately falls in behind your left leg to the admiring glances and sometimes even open applause of envious parents. Once Baby has learned to heel, it's time for it to respond to other necessary disciplines such as "Sit!", "Stay!", "Fetch!" and "Shut up!" (Some fathers enjoy also training Baby to perform cute little tricks like "rolling over" or "playing dead." I feel, however, that this tends to make Baby "show-offy" or, in extreme cases, overly friendly—an attitude that must be avoided at all costs.)

Choosing the right teaching method invariably poses a problem. Some experts encourage the carrot-and-stick approach. But I don't believe in hitting Baby with either. Instead, I advocate the use of a mildly charged cattle prod. When the little nipper declines to fetch as ordered, you merely turn up the juice, give the miscreant a little poke and, believe you me, it fetches. So, as you can see, the key to raising perfect children is to break their spirits when they're young. Once you've accomplished that, all you need say to them ever again is "Hello," "Good-bye," and "Ask your mother."

There are probably a few gentle souls who will say that these methods are perhaps a bit too callous. Nonsense. Keep in mind the essence of the parent-child relationship: It is the goal of every parent to somehow get a perfect child, and it is the goal of every child to somehow get even. A classic example of this phenomenon is a struggling author I know named Fairbough Wren. How vividly I recall the day I ran into Fairbough at a literary lunch. He looked like death warmed over.

"What is it, Fairbough?" I exclaimed, clutching his shoulder. "Tertiary coreopsis? Writers' block? An IRS audit?"

"Worse," he said gloomily. "I have finally written a book that both my agent and my publisher agree will be a critically acclaimed bestseller. At last I'm going to become famous."

"What's wrong with that?" I asked.

"What's wrong with that is my son, Pfester. Once

you're famous these days, you know your child is going to write a book about what a dirty rat you really are. Look at Joan Crawford's daughter. Look at Ernest Hemingway's son. Look at Aram Saroyan. How do you think Attila the Hun got such a rotten reputation? Attila II was an unscrupulous gossip, that's how. It's even tougher on modern parents. A kid who exposes his dad as a brutal, insecure, sex-mad drunk not only gets even, he gets a $50,000 advance."

"But you're not a brutal, insecure, sex-mad drunk, Fairbough," I said.

"You don't know Pfester. For fifty grand, he'd accuse me of the Lindbergh kidnapping. And lately he's taken to tagging along after me everywhere I go."

"He probably just wants to demonstrate his love for you."

"With a tape recorder? No, he's out to get me. I knew it the minute he dropped a bowling ball on my foot and pushed the button to preserve my response."

"Good grief! What did you say?"

"I said, 'To err is human, Pfester, and to forgive divine. You are herewith forgiven and please get that quote straight.' He did, too. He quoted it right back to me the next day after he smashed up the car."

"You're a saint, Fairbough," I said.

"I have to be. But it's lucky I caught him spiking my orange juice at breakfast. I was wondering why I kept falling asleep before lunch. One day we almost missed the baseball game."

"But you loathe baseball."

"That's true. But what would you think of a famous

American who doesn't take his boy to the ball games and eat Coney Island red hots even though he has an ulcer."

"I didn't know you had an ulcer, Fairbough."

"I didn't. But I got to worrying what would happen if I developed an ulcer. Pfester would say in his book that an ulcer proved his father, beneath his brave exterior, was an insecure, neurotic milksop. I worried so much about this that I developed an ulcer."

"That's a shame. Is it painful?"

"Only when I read the love letters I get every day from Boopsie."

"Who's Boopsie?"

"I'm sure it's Pfester. His book won't sell without sex."

"Well, that's the price of fame, Fairbough. And look at it this way: Now you'll live forever."

"Don't say that," groaned Fairbough. "The hope of dying before Pfester gets the goods on me is the only thing that's keeping me alive."

But wouldn't you know it? Fairbough's book was a monumental flop. Being a writer myself, I could well understand the pain and sense of loss this unhappy turn of events must have caused. Poor Pfester.

There are, to be sure, methods of raising children other than breaking their spirits. I became aware of one that achieved a brief measure of popularity a decade or so ago when I received the following card in the mail:

Bob and Carol
are pleased to announce the association of
Ted
in their new Mariage à Trois

I'm so square that I at first thought my three friends were into some kinky sexual adventure. But when I dropped around to their little white cottage behind its picket fence, I was quickly disabused.

"Good gracious," said Carol, rocking her new daughter, Alice, in her arms, "kinky sex went out in the sixties. We're into triple parenting."

"That's right," said Bob enthusiastically. "Double parenting was perfectly adequate in the old days when the wife stayed home, kept house, and raised the children. But now that both husbands and wives are working, two parents are simply not enough to go around."

"Believe me," said Carol, "it was tough to come home after a hard day performing open heart surgery to cook half the dinner, do half the housework, and then stay up half the night when little Alice had the colic."

"I suppose I could have quit my job and become a househusband," said Bob, "but I have my career as a clerk-typist to think about. That's why we were so delighted when Ted agreed to join our marriage."

"Gosh, I was eager to grab the opportunity," said Ted. "I'd always wanted to be a father, but I was afraid my extensive practice as a Jungian psychoanalyst would not afford me sufficient quality time with a child."

Over the years, I kept in touch with this little "thermonuclear family," as they liked to call their experimental union, and I must say everything went swimmingly. With three incomes, money was never a problem, and with three parents, Alice was the best-loved, best-cared-for child in the neighborhood. It looked as though triple parenting was here to stay. Everyone was happy. Bob was happy he had to change only six instead of nine of the eighteen daily diapers. Carol was happy that when she said, "Not tonight, I've got a headache," Ted would get up for the 2:00 A.M. feeding. As for Ted, he said, "I feel that this direct three-on-one parental-whole-child interaction is creating an admirable intrapersonal character development mode as well as a swell id"—which, everyone agreed, meant that Ted was happy, too.

As Alice grew, the advantages of triple parenting multiplied. Dealing with nightmares, laundry, whooping cough, tantrums, and chewed piano legs was a third less the burden that most parents face. And the times were so tolerant that only a few eyebrows were raised when it was Carol's coveted turn to stay home from the PTA meeting. Best of all was the general absence of quarrels over Alice's upbringing. Instead of shouting, such matters were settled by a simple majority vote. For example, when Alice at age three attempted to tie-dye the neighbor's cat in a bowl of pancake batter, Ted felt that she should be rewarded for such creative ingenuity in order to reinforce her superego. Instead, the democratic process locked her in her room. Parental discipline was a cinch with three parents available to tell Alice to keep her elbows off the table, stop biting her fingernails, and refrain from bringing home strange plants as who knew where they had been growing. There was also a proportional increase in parental delaying tactics, those being the tactics any reasonable parent employs every time a decision raises its ugly head. When Alice, aged nine, asked if she might enter a belly dancing contest for the benefit of the February 28th Movement,

Bob said he would first have to find out whether this was a worthy Republican cause; Ted said he would first have to determine whether freeing repressed sexuality without adequate stomach muscles was beneficial to the ego; and Carol said she would first have to determine whether Alice could get home before dark.

It was at this point that Alice rebelled. "It has been an interesting relationship, Daddy, Mommy, and Daddy," she said, solemnly shaking hands with each. "But I have applied for admission to The Little Cousins of the Forlorn Orphanage & Jute Mill where the supervision will be less strict, thereby enabling my little spirit to flower. Three parents is at least one more than any child deserves."

So triple parenting, rational though it might be, just hasn't worked out and many reasonable parents are giving thought to divorce instead. Much has been written about the plight of those little tykes whose parents have gone their separate ways. But what about the plight of those little tykes whose parents haven't? I hadn't realized the extent of the problem until the day Mordred came home from school in tears. It seems he was the only kid in his class that Christmas season who had but a single tree.

"One tree isn't enough, Mordred?" I said.

"Most of the guys get to spend Christmas Eve with their dads and Christmas Day with their moms," he said, scuffing a toe in the carpet, "or vice versa. But look at me; one lousy tree and one lousy set of presents to open. And you call that a merry Christmas?"

"I don't know, Mordred," I said. "Having a mommy

151 ——————

and a daddy who live in separate houses isn't all that great."

"No, what's really great is when both of them get re-married," he agreed. "Mort Heimerman has eight grand-parents. Boy, is he ever going to clean up at Christmas!"

I spoke to the school psychologist, Dr. Thurlow, about this. He said Mordred was obviously "culturally de-prived." His classmates clearly considered him to be an oddball, the doctor said, and made him the butt of such cruel taunts as "Nyah, nyah, you've only got one bed-room" or "We bet you've nowhere to go when your tv breaks down."

I asked the good doctor what should be done. "I think you and your wife should try to provide Mordred with at least some of the advantages of a broken home," said Dr. Thurlow thoughtfully. "You might begin by competing for his affections."

Initially, Glynda was somewhat dubious of this enter-prise, but she is competitive by nature and she soon en-tered into the spirit of the contest wholeheartedly. I began it by taking Mordred out of school three days running over Glynda's objections in order to attend a basketball game and two John Wayne retrospectives, which I said were educational. When we got back each evening, I'd suggest Mordred do his homework. Glynda, however, would want to play a couple of hours of double solitaire with him. Then she'd start to stick a pizza in the oven and whip up a couple of chocolate malts, but I'd quickly offer to take him out to the Burger Bazaar for dinner instead. I think Mordred enjoyed these scenes. I know he particularly liked my insisting he sit up with me until midnight to watch "Creature Features." He didn't lose any sleep, though, as Glynda refused to wake him until noon.

The experiment came to an end on Mordred's birthday. "Only one lousy set of presents," he muttered, glancing at the towering pile. "Why can't I have a normal family life like other kids?"

"Oh, shut up, Mordred," I said without thinking.

"Your father's right," said Glynda automatically.

"See?" cried Mordred triumphantly. "It's always two big adults against one little kid around here. Poor me."

With crystal clarity, I knew then and there that I had two choices: I could send Mordred to his room or I could do the right thing by him and sue Glynda for divorce. I sent him to his room. Call me selfish, if you will, but I simply couldn't bear the prospect of a bitter courtroom custody battle: "You take him!" "No, *you* take him!"

So there you have it. The only effective method of raising the perfect child from the parents' point of view is to break its spirit when it's young. Then you at least have a crack at winding up with what every parent considers the perfect child: a docile, obedient, Nobel Prize–winning physicist who calls you up every morning to ask your advice and who never, ever forgets your birthday.

CHAPTER ELEVEN

Sex and Other Education

UNDOUBTEDLY THE GRAVEST responsibility parents face is the education of their children. Once you have selected a mate, little can be done about your off-spring's intelligence. Only through education can you influence your children's destinies, helping to determine whether they become happy street sweepers or ulcerous tycoons. And only through education can you hand down the wisdom of a thousand generations to the one that comes next, thus continuing the human race on its uncharted course to God-only-knows-what mystic destiny. With the incredible immensity of this challenge in mind, I strongly recommend you start with sex.

There are two reasons for starting with sex: (1) a good

sex education is a requisite for success in such bellwether industries as magnesium mining, jute manufacturing, and designer jeans commercials, and (2) once you have completed giving a course in this all-important field, the rest of the curriculum is a cinch. Yet there are some parents who would dodge this issue. I was shocked to see a survey indicating that eight out of ten would prefer the schools take over this major parental function. Such cowardice is inexcusable. Leave sex education to the schools? Who wants sex in our schools? As my Sainted Mother used to say, "Get sex education out of the schools and back in the gutter where it belongs!" Besides, having already taught my own children about sex, I feel it only fair that they share this experience, when the time inevitably comes, with their children.

How well I recall the day Glynda decided Mordred and Malphasia were old enough at last to benefit from a cool, rational explanation of the sexual process—and that I was the one to do the explaining.

"You're better at explaining things," she explained, which is exactly what she said when the spare tire she was rolling up to the car got away and went through Mr. Crannich's plate glass window. "Just keep in mind that we modern parents think sex is a common, ordinary, everyday human activity, no different from washing the dishes."

"What else would I think it was?" I demanded indignantly.

So I coolly and rationally announced to the children at the dinner table that we should gather informally sometime to have a casual little chat sometime about a subject

that could possibly be of some importance to them sometime and let's-do-it-right-now-and-get-it-over-with.

"Are we in a war, Daddy?" asked Malphasia fearfully.

"What ever gave you that idea, dear, ha-ha?" I said.
"Now you go get your blackboard and some chalk—
maybe three colors of chalk—and we'll talk about a common, ordinary, everyday human activity no different from
washing the dishes."

"I'll wash the dishes," said Glynda.

I finally got the children arranged so they could best see
the blackboard and began my cool, rational lecture with
"Mordred, put down the cat!"

"Fluffy wants to hear, too," said Mordred.

"Fluffy already knows all about this," I said.

"Who told Fluffy?"

I decided to ignore both the question and the cat.
"Now, I am going to draw some common, ordinary,
everyday parts of the human body which are no different
than your ear," I said.

"That doesn't look like my ear," said Malphasia.

"Do you have a comment, too, Mordred?" I said sar-
donically.

"Godey's Garage burned down today," said Mordred.

"How would you like to wash the dishes?" I said and I
proceeded relentlessly—but coolly and rationally, mind
you.

I had gone through fifteen minutes and the entire parts
manual with diagrams and assembly instruction when
Malphasia raised her hand. "Can I go clean my room?"
she asked.

"We are just getting to the interesting part, Malphasia," I told her, "which is no different from washing the dishes and stop squirming."

I finally came to the end. My children now knew everything there was to know about sex. "Any questions?" I asked.

Mordred yawned. "Is it fun?" he inquired.

Well, you can't remember to impart all the little details like that in a cool, rational lecture. At least, I had managed to convey to them the knowledge that all we cool, rational human beings viewed sex as a common, ordinary, everyday activity no different from washing the dishes.

"Daddy," said Malphasia, looking up at me with that lovely, childlike curiosity, "how often do you and Mommy . . ."

"MIND YOUR OWN BUSINESS!" I coolly and rationally explained.

Glynda, concerned by the weeping, emerged from the kitchen wanting to know exactly what I had told Malphasia. "Not tonight," I said, pouring myself an after-dinner wallop, "I've got a headache."

To be honest, I've never been quite sure what good, if any, sex education did the children. One problem is that they're such rebels. Like most of her generation, Malphasia has always been a staunch feminist. She was one of the first on the block to burn her bra, not to mention her nylons, her curlers, her high heels, and the eastern one-third of her bedroom. "What next?" I said. In fact, I said it several hundred times. So when she came home after an evening out with her knight errant, Petrid Fentris, I lay waiting.

"Did you have a nice time?" I asked, that being parental talk for "Kindly list the misdemeanors and felonies you have committed in the past four hours."

"Oh, Daddy," she said, her cheeks flushed, "we had a ball!"

"I'll bet," I agreed nervously. "Tell me about it."

Well, it seems that she and Petrid and thirty or forty strangers of various sexes all got together in this big room and kind of fooled around doing this sort of new stuff that really everybody's doing and they had lots of fun actually and was there any peach pie left in the refrigerator?

A more naive parent might have left it there. But I recalled the evening Malphasia casually said she had stopped in Offenbach's Jewelry Emporium on the way home, and it wasn't until a process server rang the door bell two months later that I realized she had been in a car.

"Be specific, Malphasia," I said firmly. "Take it step by step."

She sighed, "Okay, Daddy," she said. "First off, Petrid took my right hand in his and I put my left arm around his neck."

"Why, for God's sake?"

"All the other girls were doing it, even that cute Martha Arguello and she's got a 3.5 average."

"In what?" I said. "And I suppose that hot-blooded young Petrid simply stood there doing nothing?"

"Oh, no. He put his right arm around me."

"Hah! And where did he put his hand?"

"Right here."

"I certainly hope so. Then what did you do?"

"Whatever he did. All the other girls were doing it."

"Good Lord! You mean to say you young women supinely did whatever the young men wanted? Next, you'll be campaigning against the ERA. I hope Petrid will still respect you after spending all evening publicly necking with you."

"I did *not* spend all evening with Petrid, Daddy. You see, every once in a while we'd swap partners. It was great. I met some real interesting guys."

I was stunned. "Are you telling me you were passed around from stranger to stranger like some cast-off, painted doll?"

Malphasia's lower lip protruded. "I was very popular, thank you," she said coolly. "As a matter of fact, several gorgeous hunks came up to tap Petrid on the shoulder so that he'd turn me over to them."

"And he didn't put up a fight?"

"He was a perfect gentleman all evening," said Malphasia, lifting her chin, "even when they dimmed the lights down real low and the tape deck was playing . . ."

"Don't tell me you do this to music?"

". . . was playing 'Good Night, ladies.' That's when he took me in his arms, I put my cheek to his and he pressed his body . . ."

I could bear no more. "Stop!" I cried. "Do you call this orgiastic new fad proper conduct for decent young people?"

"No," said Malphasia. "We call it touch dancing."

So I gave her ten bucks to go buy some heavy metal

rock records. But I didn't have much hope. And when I discussed this appalling threat with Glynda, she agreed. "I think they may have discovered the ultimate revenge," she said.

"What's that?" I asked.

Glynda took a thoughtful sip of her martini. "They're going to grow up like us," she said.

That's a depressing thought. But one mustn't despair. There are so many other all-important things to teach one's children besides sex. Besides sex, for instance, there's money. As every child psychologist will tell you, we parents must teach our kids how to handle money when they're young so they can deal with it in the real world when they grow up. Actually, teaching children to deal with money is as easy as falling off a log. We doting parents simply present Junior with five dollars on Monday along with a lengthy lecture on the importance of budgeting wisely, for this precious five dollars must last him all week. Inevitably, he blows it all defending the planet Earth from alien invaders down at the video arcade on Tuesday, begs a three-dollar advance for the ball game on Wednesday, and by Saturday he's a good ten dollars in the hole. Amid dire threats that he won't see another penny for two weeks, he visits Grandmother on Sunday and wheedles a sawbuck in commemoration of St. Swithin's Day. Financially rejuvenated, he's ready to start his career of profligacy afresh.

That is not, needless to say, the way the real world works. In order to teach Mordred how the real world works, we gave him an allowance of one hundred dollars a month when he hit his eleventh birthday. Actually, we didn't give it to him. We told him about it.

"In the real world, Mordred," I explained to him when he demanded cash on the barrelhead, "you are paid at the end of the month, not the beginning. And when you do receive your money, we shall be forced to withhold $29.78 for income taxes, unemployment insurance, union dues, and old-age survivor benefits, none of which I know you would wish to be without. Because you are a member of the family, however, your room and board will be a modest $62.50 a month, and if you budget $1.49 for clothes, $5.00 for carfare, and $1.17 for school supplies, you will have a whopping $5.06 left over with which to whoop it up."

"But I don't have any money at all to spend," complained the young lad.

"Of course you don't, Mordred," I said. "In the real world, nobody does. In the real world, everybody has one of these!"

With the air of a magician producing a rabbit or a politician describing how he will balance the budget, I presented Mordred with his very own plastic credit card. I wish you could have seen how his eyes lit up. And—liperty-lipperty—off he went to learn all there was to learn about credit cards.

On the very first day, he came home with a $6.95 T-shirt advertising a brand of beer, a $4.95 hockey puck, two budgies in a cage, and a used skateboard which he said was a steal at $10.00. And that very same evening he traipsed blithely down to the Bijou to see *Flipper Goes to*

Zimbabwe for $2.50 while consuming $3.00 worth of warm cola and popcorn soaked in butter-flavored coconut oil. Oh, what fun he had!

By month's end, Mordred was not only $144.12 in arrears, but he couldn't pay his rent. Naturally, I was forced to present him with handling charges, transaction charges, carrying charges, a late fee, and a stern notice that "we trust we may count on your prompt payment of these charges." He might have done better the second month if his bike hadn't been towed away, his lunch box hadn't been lost, and his new cocker spaniel puppy hadn't been inoculated with $88.00 worth of distemper, pellagra, and beriberi shots. But what broke his financial will to resist was the news from his orthodontist six weeks later that a decent smile would cost him $5,000.

Poor little guy. I showed him how to file for bankruptcy under chapter 11, which is certainly something any credit card holder should learn. Glynda and I then had a brief argument as to what course of action would be most helpful to him next. In the end, we merely stripped him of his credit card, thus reducing him to the customary childhood occupation of begging. But I still think we should have evicted him. I know it sounds draconian, but how else would you teach a child to handle credit cards?

I waited until Mordred was sixteen to tell him about Uncle Willoughby. At the time, I was huddled over a very, very, very long Form 1040, engaged in the annual national struggle between fear and avarice. At the moment Mordred walked in, I was weighing the risk of going to jail against a $27.80 deduction for a lunch with my brother-in-law at which we discussed tax shelters, I think.

"Sit down, sit down, dear boy," I said, glad of any postponement of such a fateful decision, "and tell me of your fondest hopes and wildest dreams."

"I want to get a job at Hogan's Auto Repair," he said, slouching into a chair, "and make some money."

I shook my head gently. "The goal in life is not to make money, Mordred," I informed him. "The goal in life is to make tax write-offs. You must not think of how to make money but rather of how to shelter money."

"I could shelter it in a bank vault," he said. "Yards of concrete, tons of steel. It'd take a hydrogen bomb to crack a shelter like that."

I smiled at such youthful naivete. "It might be safe from a mere hydrogen bomb," I said, "but not from the IRS. No, you must emulate our little family's financial genius, Uncle Willoughby."

"That old bore?" said Mordred.

"He may be a bore to you," I said, "but in monetary circles, his is an inspiring Horatio Alger story. Do you realize that at your age, Uncle Willoughby didn't have a cent? And in the following twenty years, by dint of brilliant planning, hard work, and sheer perseverance, he managed to lose more than seven million dollars on paper?"

"That's a lot," conceded Mordred grudgingly.

"It wasn't easy," I said. "I remember his first bold venture: breeding variegated Mongolian gerbils. He began with but seven of the little creatures and three hundred thousand cages. Fortunately, all seven were male, and when they eventually expired from old age and frustration, he harvested such a bonanza of depreciated assets that he became a legend in his own time."

"I'm allergic to gerbils," said Mordred.

"Then what about pushing medical research through new frontiers?" I asked. "You can take up the hopeless search for a cure to endemic coreopsis from your Uncle Willoughby, who retired from this gallant struggle only after he had exhausted every conceivable rapid write-off in the book."

"Medicine makes me sick."

"You'll think of something. But, remember, the path to financial success can be a rocky one. Even Uncle Willoughby had his failures. Who can ever forget the cinema epic he made back in the sixties, *Gone with the Wind, Part II—Rhett Strikes Back.*"

"It was a flop?"

"Unfortunately, no. Despite his superhuman efforts, it was a box-office smash—thereby forcing him to repay the IRS all the advance losses he had taken plus penalties and accrued interest."

"So he gave up tax shelters?"

"Far from it. At this very minute, your undaunted Uncle Willoughby is working on his *chef d'oeuvre,* a sexual energy converter. He figures that if he can harness only a quarter of the sexual energy now going to waste in this country, he can light every community west of the Mississippi."

For the first time, Mordred showed a smidgeon of interest. "Will it work?" he asked.

"Of course it will work," I said. "He starts off with a 40 percent alternative energy tax credit."

Despite such convincing arguments, I could tell that I'd lost Mordred. What spark was missing in the boy? Was he the pawn of ingrained laziness? Or did he lack the courage to take the risks that success demands?

"Seize the day, Mordred!" I said. "As a red-blooded American, it's your duty to take advantage of the glorious opportunities our great free-enterprise system offers."

"Heck, Dad," said Mordred, "it seems simpler to just make the money and pay what you owe."

I discussed this conversation later with Glynda. In her maternal tolerance, she ascribed Mordred's attitude to the callowness of youth. But I was far from convinced. "You know what I think?" I said. "I think the kid's a commie."

Once you have attempted to instruct your children in the use of credit cards and tax shelters, you can complete their financial education with brief instructions on how they must stand back five feet and look nonchalantly the other way when the person in front of them in line is punching a secret code into the automatic sidewalk teller. All this, of course, is for the benefit of the child.

In keeping with the spirit of this book, let us now discuss how to educate the child for the benefit of the parent. The first priority here is to help your little ones with their homework. I became aware of this critical need the day I heard hammering next door. I stuck my head out the window and there was my neighbor Mr. Crannich, pounding a FOR SALE sign into his lawn.

"You're not giving up that home you love and cherish

so dearly, are you, Crannich?" I asked with grave concern.

"Have to," he said gloomily. "We've been struck with a financial disaster of incredible magnitude and we're not insured."

"Flood? Earthquake? Holocaust?" I hazarded. Although I hadn't seen any evidence of such in the neighborhood lately, little else would account for Crannich's demeanor.

"Worse than that. It's our son, Herschel. We have to raise $50,000."

"The poor kid," I said. "Don't tell me he needs a delicate operation by a Viennese podiatrist or he'll never play the piano again."

"Worse than that."

"Worse than that? I tried to conceive the most awesome financial disaster imaginable. "I know! He ran over Melvin Belli with the family car."

"Worse than that," said Crannich, shaking his head hopelessly. "He's been admitted to Harvard."

"Good Lord!" I cried. For this was the catastrophe every middle-class American family dreads. "Where did you, as parents, go wrong?"

"That's just the question the wife and I have been asking ourselves," Crannich said. "Heaven only knows we did our best to see that he would achieve an enviable straight C average that would insure his entering a cheap junior college."

"There, there, Crannich," I said. "I'm sure it's not your fault. Maybe he just fell in with the right crowd."

"Oh, no, we screened his friends very carefully. I remember once we caught him trying to sneak out on a date with the Homecoming Queen of the Scholarship Society. Naturally, we put a quick stop to that."

"Naturally. But, still, these youngsters do tend to emulate their peer groups."

"I know. That's why he was the first kid on the block to have a Harley-Davidson. And his mother sat up all night riveting 'Born to Lose' on the back of the black leather jacket we gave him for Christmas."

"You can't beat that for parental devotion," I agreed. "It seems to me the schools are to blame. You never know when these teachers are putting ideas into our children's heads."

"We did our best to counteract that by providing an ideal home environment," said Crannich. "Not once did we help him with his homework. What beats me is how a boy who's required to watch five hours of television every night can get straight A's in anything."

"Well, cheer up, Crannich," I said. "With luck, he may flunk out of Harvard in his freshman year and become a plumber."

"That's too much to hope for. We're looking on the bright side, though. We figure that if we sell everything we own, we'll just barely manage to get him through the first three years. After that, we'll be on easy street."

"How's that?"

"We'll be so poor," said Crannich, "that he'll qualify for. a scholarship."

Any expert parent will have immediately spotted Crannich's incredible error. Where he failed, of course, was in not helping Herschel with his homework. When I think of the long hours I spent patiently tutoring Mordred and Malphasia, all I can say is that it was well worth it. Could I help it if they changed the dates of the First Punic War since I was in school? (I think it was due to the shift to the Gregorian calendar.) Is it my fault that some overly tolerant pedant generously granted "eiderdown" an exemption from the rule of "i before e except after c"? And surely the question of whether or not both sides wouldn't have been better off if the South had won the Civil War is a matter of opinion. How could I know his American history teacher hailed from Birmingham?

Be that as it may, thanks to my dedication in helping Mordred and Malphasia with their assignments, neither even thought of applying to Harvard. So the effort I put into tutoring them paid off a good ten grand apiece, for they were barely accepted by Hiram Skarewe University, a well-endowed public institution known for its well-endowed co-eds, its well-endowed winter sports program, and a spirited football cheer. Needless to say, once they no longer were required to appear nightly before a parental judge and jury at the dinner table, both promptly rebelled.

Mordred did so by refusing to join a fraternity. "I don't like getting drunk" was the only excuse he had to offer.

"Look, Mordred," I said, "fraternities are back in vogue. You will make friendships that will stand you in good stead all your life."

"Beer makes me feel bloated," said Mordred.

"And the memories will remain with you until your

dying day. As you stand in the gloaming with your sworn brothers serenading the beautiful young women in the sorority house next door, you will find yourself taking in all that is warm and good and do you know the effect that will have on you?"

"I'll throw up," said Mordred.

There was no persuading him otherwise. Just to spite us, he moved into a dorm with a bunch of other social misfits, refused to learn to ski, and maintained a 3.6 grade-point average.

Malphasia's rebellion took a different turn. It surfaced the first weekend she came home and boldly told us of her plunge. "I have enrolled in a broad curriculum of rewarding courses that will ensure my emerging from my chrysalis of youthful ignorance as a well-rounded human being."

"Good," I said. "I trust that means you are majoring in gene splicing and minoring in computer programming?"

"No, I am majoring in comp lit as I am interested in sixteenth-century Italianate villanelles and minoring in Etruscan libation urns," she said, "as I feel this will best prepare me for life."

"As a Zen nun?" I asked.

But it was all to no avail. Malphasia was determined to fritter away four years and forty thousand of our dollars poring over the works of Herodotus, Congreve, and Proust. Every once in a while, I'd send her the help-wanted ads with a scribbled notation: "Look, not one single opening for a comp lit operator."

As usual where the children were concerned, Glynda

looked on the bright side. "I think perhaps Malphasia is the forerunner of a trend back to the glories and rewards of academic learning for learning's sake."

"She'll be an unemployed bum," I said gloomily.

"True," said Glynda, "but she'll be a *well-educated* unemployed bum."

Getting your children into college is often a difficult problem. Another that parents frequently must face is getting them out. When Mordred's four years were up, the country was in the midst of a recession. The administration of Skarewe University looked forward to the commencement ceremonies with some trepidation. And rightly so. The trouble began during the commencement address, which was entitled, "From These Failing Hands We Fling the Torch." It was delivered by President Hiram A. Skarewe IV, who began, "As you go forth today from these cloistered halls . . ."

President Skarewe said later that the only reason he stopped dead at this point was that he could think of nothing further to say. The somewhat awkward silence was finally broken by a group of activists in the back rows who folded their arms, sat in the aisles and began chanting, "Hell no; we won't go!"

At first, President Skarewe attempted to plead with them. "Look, it won't be too bad," he wheedled. "Some of you may even find jobs, if you are members of a minority group and of the female persuasion."

When this proved ineffectual, Skarewe resorted to force. "Aardvale, James," he called out, reading from the class roster. Campus police promptly overpowered James

Aardvale, twenty-one, and carried him kicking and screaming up to the rostrum where President Skarewe said, "Congratulations, Aardvale," as decorum demanded, and served him with his diploma. Aardvale was then thrown bodily out the Main Gate with a stern warning not to return under penalty of arrest.

Aardvale's example, unfortunately, served to panic the remainder of the graduating class. They fled in all directions, shedding caps and gowns, overturning the Martha Skarewe Memorial Bench, and demolishing the traditional daisy chain. The largest group holed up in the Albert Skarewe Botany Building and announced a list of forty-seven "non-negotiable demands"—the first and foremost being recognition of their right not to graduate if they didn't want to. With admirable firmness, President Skarewe had them routed from the building with tear gas and herded them out the gate with fire hoses.

Others chained themselves to radiators and trees. Minerva Quillby, a shapely blonde, doffed her clothes and attempted to pose as a fourth water nymph supporting the baroque seashell in the Lotta M. Skarewe Commemorative Fountain. This earned her a bad cold and a tryout for the centerfold in *Playboy*. The rare employment opportunity elated Miss Quillby. "I owe my entire career," she later told *People* magazine, "to my college education."

After seventy-two hours, President Skarewe said confidently he felt the commencement ceremonies were about over as all but three members of the graduating class had been rounded up and heaved out. "If conditions on the outside don't improve," he said privately, "I shall urge that we replace next year's commencement exercises with a surprise fire drill."

But, I'm glad to say, conditions did improve, and at this writing, many young people are actually anxious to leave the serene, secure, joy-filled groves of academe to pursue their careers in the real world. I can't for the life of me see why.

CHAPTER TWELVE

Value Your Child

Eventually, IF THINGS break right, your precious offspring will reach the age of twenty-one and will fly off from the nest. Unfortunately, they usually still call you up occasionally to say hello and ask for bail money. This is where the Planned Parenthood Retirement Plan comes in.

With the advent of simple, effective contraceptive devices in the 1960s, it became clear that the major problem of parenthood was no longer avoiding having unwanted children. It was getting rid of the unwanted children you already had. Being a parent, all parents agree, is a tough, nerve-jangling ulcer-producing job, comparable to working in a boiler factory. Yet the boilermaker enjoys one tremendous advantage over the parent: No matter how harried or bored or frustrated he is during his long hours of drudgery, he can solace himself with golden dreams of that happy day when he will retire, leaving the boiler factory behind forever to devote his remaining years to his own pleasures and pursuits. But the parent! Since the dawn of time, parents have been granted no such benefits. Their only release from their grueling job was issued, I shudder to say, by the Grim Reaper.

The new Planned Parenthood Retirement Plan—still on the drawing board, I fear—will do much to correct these inequities. True, parents won't get back a penny of the thousands upon thousands of dollars they've spent on their little ones. And, true, they won't receive even an inadequate pension. But they will have the retirement benefit they deserve most of all: retirement.

As I see it, a simple, little ceremony will take place on the child's twenty-first birthday: "I want you to accept this suitably inscribed gold watch in appreciation of your twenty-one years of loyal, dedicated service to me," says the child. "Frankly, I don't know what I would have done without you."

"Thank you," says the father. "I know I speak for your mother, too, when I say what great pleasure this occasion brings. During the twenty-one years we worked for you, there were some trying times, beginning with diaper rash and colic, extending through the usual childhood diseases, two expulsions from school, three arrests, and, of course, 7,304 attempts to get you to clean up your room, which, by the way, we have now simply walled up. But there

have also been many rewards, I'm sure, and I would like
to cite an example, if only I could think of one. So now
that we are retired, your mother and I plan to devote our
new leisure time to worthy causes. Our first will be to join
the fight to lower the Planned Parenthood Retirement age
to eighteen. Thank you."

Unhappily, the Planned Parenthood Retirement Plan
is still undergoing pilot tests in Pierre, South Dakota.
Until it is readily available, I would strongly urge you to
consider running a want ad similar to the one I composed
for Mordred:

> FOR SALE
> Male Child, 21
> Gd. cond. Full equip. Low Maint.
> $50,000. Firm

Let me make one thing perfectly clear: I did not place
that classified ad in the paper simply because Mordred
put me on hold. I will admit that nothing makes a man
feel more over the hill than when his son puts him on
hold. He had called me from his office where he was serving as temporary vacation relief for the night watchman
to discuss a small loan when there was a click and he said,
"Just a minute, Dad; I've got another call." I sat looking
at the receiver and thinking of the time he loutishly lost
the spinnaker sheet on our fourteen-foot sailboat as we
were leading on the homeward leg of the all-important
Silas Thurgood Memorial Race and I somehow refrained
from hitting him with the canoe paddle. O, how sharper
than a serpent's tooth!

But I am not a vengeful person. The reason I placed that classified ad was a simple matter of economics. I just saw no reason not to take advantage of the current boom in adult child sales sweeping the country.

As I told the first prospects to come calling, Melissa and Burgess Bindler-Sander "Mordred's a steal at only $50,000. I've got a lot more than that in him."

"I don't know," said Melissa dubiously. "I've always sort of hoped, Burgess, that we could have a child of our own."

"Are you out of your skull?" said Burgess. "I read just the other day that we'd have to shell out $250,000 to raise a new infant to the age of eighteen, much less twenty-one. Heck, Melissa, that's ten Maseratis."

"And that doesn't include the cost of a college education," I said helpfully. "By 1998, with the current rate of inflation, that should come to at least another $100,000. The only reason I can let you have Mordred at such a low price is that kids were a lot cheaper in his day."

"Has he had all his shots?" asked Burgess cautiously.

"You bet," I said. "And, needless to say, he's house-broken. I suppose you know that chore alone occupies the parents' first two years."

"Can you imagine some squawling infant drooling all over our Flokati rugs, pulling the leaves off our ficus and knocking over our sound system?" demanded Burgess of Melissa.

"Speaking of sound systems," I said slyly, "with the money you save on orthodontists alone, you could buy a Bang & Olufsen."

"Wow!" said Burgess. "And you mentioned 'low maintenance' in your ad."

"That's right," I said. "He's stopped growing so you won't have to buy him new shoes every three months. And, when it comes to feeding him, you'd think he'd come to dinner once a week. But, believe me, he won't."

"You also said he was fully equipped," said Burgess. "I assume that means a wardrobe, a car, and a room of his own someplace?"

"Certainly," I said. "And he's also had piano, bowling, and driving lessons. If you don't think driving lessons are important, I'll be glad to show you all the bills from the body shop."

"That settles it," said Burgess. "No kid of mine is going to learn to drive in my Maserati."

"But, Burgess," protested Melissa, "you don't have a Maserati."

"I will have," said Burgess, happily rubbing his palms together in anticipation, "after I've saved a third of a million dollars by buying a full-grown son."

Melissa gave it one last try. "Let's think it over, Burgess," she said. "You know I've always wanted to hear the pitter-patter of little feet around the house."

"But that's the beauty of it, Melissa," said Burgess. "Mordred will be getting married soon. So we'll be grandparents with none of the headaches and drudgery of raising children. And, best of all, he'll have to pay to bring them up!"

Well, that convinced Melissa, and I pocketed Burgess's check. I'll miss Mordred. He was a good son in many

ways, even if he did put me on hold. But it's certainly
gratifying to get my investment back. I didn't have the
heart to tell Burgess and Melissa about Mordred's plans.
It's true he's going to get married. Like most young people
in these incredibly expensive times, however, he's already
saving up to buy a full-grown kid of his own.

I'm also glad Burgess and Melissa didn't ask me what
career goals Mordred had chosen to pursue after his grad-
uation from college. For, at the time, he had decided to
run for president. Oh, the shame of it all!

God knows Glynda and I did everything we could to see
that he became a smashing success, or at least enough of a
success to support us in our old age. We read him a steady
diet of Horatio Alger stories when he was a tad to instill in
him that old-fashioned American get-up-and-go. And
when we had finished, he would invariably get up and go
turn on the tv. We tried not to push him. I can't remember how many times I told him, "We don't care what you
become as long as you're happy, Mordred, so why don't
you get your act together, for heaven's sake, and become a
doctor?"

But Mordred lacked the hand-eye coordination to become a skilled surgeon who could sink a twelve-foot putt
on Wednesday afternoon.

"Maybe he'll become a distinguished lawyer," said
Glynda optimistically.

"You know he can't stand the sight of money," I said.
"Besides, I doubt if he could ever pass the bar. Any bar."

Mordred's first interest was in becoming a fireman, and
I must say that he threw his heart into it. In his initial in-

terview he was asked why he wanted to join the department. "Oh, I love fires!" Mordred said breathlessly. "I love seeing those devouring flames licking ever upward, insatiably consuming all in their path as the soft black smoke billows. . . ." It was one of the few entrance tests he didn't flunk; they wouldn't let him take it.

Among the tests Mordred did flunk were those for post office mail sorter (weak on alphabetizing), practical nurse (not too practical), city hall draftsman (philosophically opposed to drafting), and nursery school teacher (I didn't ask). Our final effort was to send Mordred down to take the Mullholland Multiphasic Vocational Determinator Test, in which he was asked all sorts of penetrating questions like, "Do you take cream in your coffee?" Batteries of psychologists, we were told, would pore over his answers and after long consultations would be able to inform him precisely what vocation he should choose in order to lead a happy, productive life. When he came home that day, Glynda and I were eagerly waiting to hear what career he would pursue. "What is it to be, Mordred?" I cried. "Merchant prince? Astro-physicist? Ambassador at large?"

"I flunked," said Mordred.

"That does it, Mordred," I said, throwing up my hands. "There's no job in this world that requires no tests, no experience, no need to read or write, or no educational, physical, or intelligence standards."

"There's one, Dad," said Mordred.

Oh, the shame of it all!

Fortunately, running for president was only a phase he

was passing through. Once he had been roundly defeated, we had one last man-to-man talk about his career. "In the final analysis, Dad," he said, "I've decided to dedicate myself to a life of crime."

"Crime! You're out of your mind, Mordred. What kind of a career is that?"

"An exciting, challenging, rewarding one, I hope, Dad. Money, leisure, travel . . ."

"You're forgetting one thing, son. Crime doesn't pay . . ."

"Nonsense, Dad."

". . . the way it used to."

"I'm sure I can make a decent living at it, Dad, if I work hard and apply myself."

"Your trouble, son, is that you're an incurable romantic. You think crime's still the way it was back in the good old days when we had folk heroes like Bonnie and Clyde, John Dillinger, Ma Barker, and Al Capone. Living legends they were. Yes, sir, when it came to crime, the whole world thought of America as the land of opportunity."

"There's still a chance for an ambitious young man out there, Dad."

"Even the cops were better, son. J. Edgar Hoover, Elliot Ness, Dick Tracy. Name me one nationally recognized crime-fighter today. And, heavens to Betsy, how long has it been since we've had an eight-state manhunt or even a cheap local dragnet?"

"So what, Dad?"

"The point, son, is that no field of American endeavor has sunk lower in recent years than crime. From its peak of greatness in the thirties, it's deteriorated into a shoddy, seamy, tawdry occupation plied only by pimply-faced punks, shakey-handed hopheads, and assorted derelicts."

"That's a pretty narrow-minded view, Dad."

"Oh, is it? Look at bank robberies. In the good old days, the black, low-slung sedan would pull up to the curb. Six guys in overcoats carrying Tommy guns would leap out and take over the whole bank. 'Shut up and no one gets hurt!' the leader would shout. They would stuff stacks of money into an attache case and with a squeal of burning rubber and the rat-a-tat-tat of police bullets make their exciting getaway. But today? Today, it's one sleazy character in a dirty ski jacket who sidles up to the teller with a hand-scrawled note. And what's he invariably carrying? A brown paper bag. Criminy, son, he isn't even wearing a tie!"

"Clothes aren't everything, Dad."

"It's not only the lack of prestige, son. You have to think of the financial rewards. Take your common, ordinary, everyday mugger. Do you realize the average little old lady carries only $2.08 in her purse? This means you have to mug three little old ladies an hour just to make ends meet."

"I don't care all that much about money, Dad."

"That's what you young idealists always say. But wait till you get out there and discover the sheer drudgery of a life of crime. Believe you me, son, you mug one little old lady and you've mugged them all."

"Dad, there's no point in arguing. I've already accepted a position as a management trainee."

"In what specialty? Burglary, armed robbery, auto theft. . . ."

"No, Dad, as a junior accountant with the Glutco, Incorporated, conglomerate."

"Oh, thank God, son, *that* kind of crime!"

As you might expect, Malphasia presented her own problems. It seems like only yesterday that she came down to breakfast in a swirling pink chiffon gown and wide-brimmed Florentine straw hat. "Good morning, Father; good morning, Mother," she said, favoring us with a little curtsy. "It is a lovely day, is it not?"

Glynda and I exchanged an uneasy glance. There could be no doubt. Our only daughter, hitherto a normal, over-sexed, pot-smoking American kid, had fallen victim to an addiction sweeping this once-virile nation—romance novels. Oh, I know a number of well-meaning liberals contend that romance novels are naught but a harmless diversion—less debilitating than heroin, less fattening than alcohol, and at $3.50 a copy, far less expensive, when it comes to providing a high, than cocaine. But this thesis overlooks the insidious appeal of the vice to today's young woman. There she is, sorely challenged by demands that she prove her equality in the dog-eat-dog marketplace and justly terrified by the threat of an impending nuclear war. And here is a chance to escape for an hour or so into a fantasy world wherein her worst fear is that the villain will steal a kiss. And she knows she will be saved in the final chapter by the Twelfth Duke of Something-or-Other, who promises to take loving care of her forever and ever, which sure beats the welfare state. Is it any wonder we are in danger of turning out a generation of females with heads filled with whipped cream?

So I was understandably stern when I turned to Malphasia. "I take it from your costume that you're not going to work today," I said. "What about your career?"

"I am renouncing clerk-typing, dear Father," she said, "for fear I might break a fingernail, thus incapacitating me from painting flower arrangements, playing Chopin, finishing my needlework, and singing 'The Farmer's Daughter's Lament,' as well as other popular songs. And now, if you will forgive me, I shall retire to the garden to pluck a fresh bouquet of primulas for dear Miss Mimmsey next door, who, I fear, suffers from the ague."

"Don't be so hard on the girl," said Glynda after Malphasia had flounced out. "She's merely searching for security."

"If it's security she wants," I growled, "I'll buy her a can of Mace."

But what could we do? We tried the obvious cures, such as substituting television soap operas for romance novels. But every time adultery, incest, or abortion was mentioned, Malphasia would swoon. And it certainly wasn't doing her much good spending six hours a day on the living room floor with the vapors. True, that was time that she wasn't locked in her room arranging her "toilette," as she put it (rather indelicately, I thought). But—hah!—I knew what she was *really* up to. A quick fix, that's what. And, sure enough, hidden under all her new elbow-length white gloves I found a stash of paperbacks with such titles as *Windswept Love* and *Daphne and the Marquis.* Naturally, I confronted her and demanded to know what we were going to do about her.

"You might send me to visit an aunt in Venice, dear Father," she said. "That is the course Gardenia's parents wisely pursued when they mistakenly feared that the Twelfth Duke of Something-or-Other, who loved her madly, was a rake."

"You don't have an aunt in Venice, damn it!" I told her. "Get yourself down to the Asparagus Fern Bar & Grill and don't come home without a red-blooded, beer-drinking, hairy-chested male chauvinist."

She was back two hours later with a handsome, steely-eyed fellow in tow. "This is Robert, Father," she said demurely. And I could tell from the look in her eye that Robert was just the guy to save her from her sordid addiction and sweep her back into the hard world of reality.

"Glad to meet you, Bob," I said, cheerily pumping his mitt. "And what do you do?"

"I am the Twelfth Duke of Something-or-Other," he said. "And I have come to ask for your daughter's hand in marriage so that I may take loving care of her forever and ever."

Curses! But it all ended happily. For it turned out that Robert was not only a complete phony but also a dedicated rake. Malphasia was so broken-hearted that she gave her pink chiffon gown to the poor, donated her collection of eighteenth-century harpsichord records to the homeless, and took a vow of lifelong poverty. "I will devote my time on this earth to serving humanity," she said nobly.

While not particularly religious, I couldn't help but be impressed. "Somehow I never thought of you as a saint, Malphasia," I said. "But here you are, preparing for a life of poverty as a nun . . ."

"A nun?" said Malphasia. "I'm preparing myself for a life of poverty as a teacher."

Now I was *really* impressed. "You mean you're willing to break up fist fights, blow noses, and clean out gerbil cages for a lousy $250 a week?" I said. "Malphasia, you *are* a saint!"

But after hearing what a beginning teacher makes, Malphasia discovered she wasn't *that* dedicated. And she decided to serve humanity by following in her brother's footsteps as a management trainee for the Glutco, Inc., conglomerate. "After all, Daddy," she explained to me patiently, "Glutco stockholders are humanity, too."

But children do grow up. They do leave home. They do set out to lead lives of their own, generally at your expense. One of the first parents in recorded history to cope successfully with this problem was Harmsweigh Potter. I hope the example he set will stand you in good stead when your turn comes. Potter's turn came when his son, Stewart, announced that he wished to leave the family nest. "I have finished college, and it is high time I at last pushed aside the sheltering wings of parental security and soared forth to make my own way in the world," Stewart informed his father. "Can you afford $500 a month for this swell apartment I found?"

Like most parents, Potter viewed the request with mixed emotions. On the one hand, it would be pleasant to

Arthur Hoppe

come home and not find Stewart with his feet up on the coffee table listening to The Ebullient Zombies singing "You Screwed Up My Love" while eating the very last piece of cold leg of lamb that Potter had carefully saved from his dinner the night before. On the other hand, Potter had spent twenty-one years dealing with Stewart's afflictions from diaper rash to that girl he went scuba diving with last summer. And now Stewart was finally fit and free to mow the lawn, empty the garbage, and otherwise repay a small share of the energy that had been invested in him. So Potter gave the matter considerable thought.

"You are absolutely right, Stewart," he said, after a full week of contemplation. "It is time you were on your own, learning to deal with the challenges of adult living—like remembering to lock all the doors before you go to bed."

"Thanks, Dad," said Stewart with a happy smile. "But, don't worry, this apartment's only got one door and it locks automatically."

"You must also learn," said Potter, "to pick up the soggy shopping flyers on the front steps, scoop the dog leavings off the sidewalk and change a thirty-amp fuse in total darkness without electrocuting yourself."

"I think the janitor takes care of all those nagging chores, Dad."

"There is nothing that will better teach you patience and humility," said Potter thoughtfully, "than waiting for the washing machine repairman. Only a mature adult who has found his peace with God can devote two weeks to such a retreat without losing his sanity."

——— 188

"The washing machine's in the basement, Dad. You just stick a quarter in it when you want to use it. So I won't have to bother with that."

"Think of the tact, diplomacy, and discretion you will inevitably acquire," said Potter, pressing on indefatigably, "by constantly dealing with people at the door selling religion, Girl Scout cookies, and Little League tickets. Yes, you'll develop responsibility remembering to stop the paper when you go on vacation, depth perception trimming the hedges, and perseverance in arguing over high electric bills."

"Look, Dad," said Stewart, who was getting a bit tired of the whole thing, "the apartment's on the sixth floor and utilities are included. In fact, I don't see where anyone living there would face these headaches you're talking about."

"Exactly, son," said Potter cheerfully. "And that's why your mother and I have decided that, in order to build your character, we'll be moving into your apartment instead. Here are the keys to the house and happy coping."

I must say that Mr. and Mrs. Potter are quite content in their new, carefree life style. They do wish Stewart would stop pestering them, though. He keeps pleading with them to come home.

But far worse than a child's urge to leave home to live is its urge to come home to live, bringing its spouse and kids with it. I hadn't realized the poignancy of this problem until the night I found my friend Timmish standing on my doorstep, suitcase in hand, looking forlorn and desperate. "Can you put me up for a couple of nights?" he asked. "I'm on my way to raft down the Monongahela single-handed."

"When did you decide to embark on a hazardous adventure like that?" I inquired.

"About twenty minutes ago," he said, "when I discovered that, for the third time this week, little Timmy hadn't bothered to refill the ice trays."

"Little Timmy's come home?" I said. "How lovely for you."

"That's easy for you to say," said Timmish. "But he's come home with his wife, Cosmic Birdsong, and their toddler, Tiny Tim." He suddenly clutched my arm. "You won't tell them that I'm here, will you?"

I experienced a twinge of nostalgia. "Do you know," I said, "those are exactly the words little Timmy used the night he knocked on my door back in '74. I remember having a long talk with him about how you can't run away from your problems."

Timmish backed off. "I suppose that's what you're going to tell me, too," he said defensively.

"Look, Timmish, I wouldn't give you advice," I said. "You're a mature adult and if you want to duck out on your responsibilities, you must have a good reason."

"Milk glasses," said Timmish, nodding glumly. "Little Timmy forgets to rinse out his milk glasses and they have that sticky ring in the morning. Why does he never remember to rinse out his milk glasses?"

"He never did, did he?"

"No, but how can I send a twenty-eight-year-old man to his room? You wouldn't believe how frustrating it is to have a grown child as a houseguest. He leaves the tv on all night and I can't even raise my voice. And Cosmic Bird-song's even more difficult. She pays no attention to me whatsoever."

"Don't tell me she's still anti-establishment in this day and age."

"She's sure anti-my-establishment," said Timmish. "Who else would put a lipstick in the clothes drier, try to cook s'mores in the toaster oven, or call the Pismo Beach Sheriff's Office long distance to ask if the clams are running?"

"You might as well get around to Tiny Tim," I said.

"Who else," he said without pausing for breath, "would free the guppies, roll in my iris bed, and eat the ficus? The kid's a thrip. And can I even mention his swaths of destruction? No, I've got to bottle it all up inside with my ulcer. Take it from me, being a parent the second time around is a thousand times more frustrating than the first."

"You really think so?" I said.

Timmish grimaced. "It's hard enough dealing with a kid," he said, "when you can shout at it."

But, more often than not, they don't come home. Not even on Sundays. Is that too much to ask? No, they don't come home. They lead their own lives equipped with the genes and lessons you gave them. They are a test of you. Their successes are your successes; their failures your failures. Some will lead their lives to the fullest; most will lead lives of noisy desperation. As a parent, I can't help but wonder if I made the right choices for my children. What are the right choices? Where will it all end?

Scene: *The Heavenly Waiting Room. Two men are seated reading magazines. One, Buck Ace, handsome, silver-haired, craggy-jawed and tanned, is leafing through* The National Geographic. *The other, Stanley Stockstill, gray, paunchy, and bespectacled, is studying an ad for a power mower in* House and Garden.

ACE: Good article in here on Pago Pago. I remember sailing in there just at sunrise on a battered old copra schooner when I was a kid of twenty-three. Ever been out to the South Pacific, Stockstill?

STOCKSTILL: No. No, I can't say that I have. Betty— that's my wife—Or I guess I should say my widow—Anyway, Betty and I talked about a trip to Bora Bora when we were first married. But then the kids started coming along . . .

ACE (*without much interest*): How many did you have?

STOCKSTILL: Three. They're all married now. I've even got two grandchildren. Here's their picture.

ACE: Very nice. Frankly, there have been times when I wished I had kids. But as I said to my second wife, Brenda, the purpose of life is to live it to the fullest. And you can't do that if you're saddled with children.

STOCKSTILL: No. No, I suppose not.

ACE: I spent my thirties traipsing around Europe as a war correspondent. I wish you could've seen Paris in those days. Ah, sipping Pernod in the Montmartre. Or running the bulls in Pamplona. I'll never forget moonrise over the Grand Canal on my thirty-second birthday.

STOCKSTILL: That's funny. I'll never forget my thirty-second birthday either. Betty had baked the cake and we were just waiting for Jennie, our second child, to come home when the phone rang. She'd been hit by a bus as she left dancing school. She was in a coma for a week. We thought for sure we were going to lose her. Then one evening, she opened her eyes and ... Well, anyway, she's fine. But enough of that. What did you do after Europe?

ACE: Started a public relations firm in Manhattan. I love that city: drinks at the Algonquin, dinner at Twenty-One, opening night at the latest Broadway musical.... That's living life to the hilt. What do you think of New York, Stockstill?

STOCKSTILL: We've only been there once. Took Stanley Junior when he was five. I remember he poured ink all over our hotel room. I could've killed him. But I must say he turned out great. (*proudly*) He's a cardiologist in Miami.

ACE: Oh? We used to winter in Palm Beach. Spent our summers in Majorca. Ever been to ...

STOCKSTILL (*wistfully*): No. No, we never got anywhere much, what with having to put three kids through college. Then, just between us, our youngest, Mary, got hooked on drugs during the sixties. It cost us a fortune to straighten her out. She's fine now. Teaches kindergarten in Chicago. But we were just getting out of debt. In fact, only last night Betty was talking about our perhaps taking a trip to Europe next year and now ...

ACE (*sympathetically*): I've always said you go through life only once. But maybe you'll be lucky. Maybe they'll send you back for another chance.

193 ——————

(*St. Peter enters, perusing his Golden Book*)

ST. PETER: Come right in, sir. You have indeed lived life to the fullest.

ACE (*rising*): Thank you.

ST. PETER: Not you, sir. You, Mr. Stockstill. For you have experienced the depths of anger, hate, shame, and fear as well as the heights of love, hope, pride, and joy. One surely cannot live life more fully than that, can one?

ACE: But what about me?

ST. PETER (*checking the Golden Book*): You, Mr. Ace? Oh, we're sending you back for another chance. And this time, I do hope you do it right.

CHAPTER THIRTEEN

The Generation Gap
& Let's Keep It That Way

MUCH HAS BEEN written about the Generation Gap, such a yawning chasm in the sixties, and how it has gently closed in recent years as our children have become more like us. There is a modicum of truth in this or perhaps even a modicum and a half, but no more than that. Take the well-documented case of Simon Lightfoot, who, like any enterprising young man in the sixties, tossed bricks through the windows of mom-and-pop sandwich shops in order to end the war in Vietnam. It was while attempting to unfurl a Viet Cong banner atop the campus flagpole during the celebration of the Tet offensive that Simon fell on his noggin, thereby lapsing into a coma from which he recovered only the other day. His elated parents were at his bedside to hear his first words, which were, of course, "Down with the Establishment!"

"There, there, Simon," said his father. "Try to keep calm . . ."

"Oh, it's you, Dad," said Simon. "Look, I don't care what your generation says. The Establishment got us into this mess in Vietnam and the only thing to do is admit our mistake and withdraw our troops, even if it means letting the Communists take over."

"Please, Simon," said his mother, "we already did that."

"No (bleep)?" said Simon unbelievingly. Then he caught himself. "Sorry to use a four-letter word in front of you, Mom," he said, "but you know how we members of the Dirty-Word Movement feel about the Establishment's irrational prudery."

"Oh, that's all right, Simon," said his mother. "Many women say (bleep), (bleep), and even (bleep-bleep) these days."

"They do?" said Simon, wincing. "That's nice." Then he added defiantly, "But no matter what you think, I'm not going to cut my hair."

"It looks lovely, Simon," said his mother. "It's not as long as your father's was in the seventies, but . . ."

"Dad, you let your hair grow long?"

"Just for a couple of years, son," said his father. "Then the kids cut theirs, and we cut ours, and long hair's out of vogue now. As I was saying to your sister, Beth, when she came over to dinner the other night . . ."

"You had Beth to dinner?" said Simon. "Well, I'm glad you finally forgave her for running off with that guy to live in a commune. I guess that means you forced him to marry her in order to conform with your ridiculous Establishment conventions."

"Oh, no, Simon," said his father. "They're still just living together. Some young people get married these days and some don't. It's purely a matter of personal preference. But he's doing well. He has a chain of adult theaters and just joined the Chamber of Commerce."

Simon was beginning to look slightly dazed. "Now you're going too far," he said. "There's no conceivable way the Establishment could get rid of its thoroughly ingrained sexual hangups and realize that obscenity is simply in the mind of the beholder because . . ."

"Don't shout, Simon," said his mother nervously. "Why don't you just curl up with a magazine and get a good rest?"

Unfortunately, the magazine Simon chose to curl up with was *Playboy*. He took one look at the centerfold, gasped a few words, and lapsed back into his coma. But his parents assume he's happier that way. For the few words he gasped were a paraphrase of Pogo's perceptive remark: "We have met the Establishment," he murmured as his eyes closed, "and they are us."

And I think Simon's parents may be right. Simon's at least happier than his contemporary, Reuben Hoffman, whom I ran into down at the hardware store. Reuben, who attempted to end the draft single-handedly by setting fire to the Phoebe Bostwick Skarewe Zoology Building, is now a thirty-six-year-old marketing analyst. He looked, I'm pleased to say, terrible.

"It's my fifteen-year-old son, Freedom Train," said

Reuben, moodily examining a tube of bathtub caulk. "Not only does he want to join the ROTC but he's decided to change his name to Jason."

"It's a good, honest name," I said.

Reuben ignored me. "His only goals in life," he said, "are a condo, a Porsche, and high-tech job with a golden parachute."

I relished that for a moment. "And I suppose he finds anyone over thirty untrustworthy?" I asked hopefully.

"No, he finds anyone under $30,000 a year untrustworthy. He finds anyone over thirty to be simply superfluous. It isn't that he doesn't trust my opinions, he just thinks they're not relevant any more. At the hint of tofu, he screams. All he wants is Wonder bread, Velveeta, and fruit pies. Wonder bread! And to think that my generation fought and bled for the nine-grain loaf and Jarlsberg cheese."

"Not so loud, Reuben," I said nervously. "You don't want to create a scene."

"Of course not," he said, pulling himself together. "But what I can't bear is his attitude toward music. Imagine lumping Frank Sinatra and Mick Jagger together."

"Imagine!" I agreed. "Who's Mick Jagger?"

"When I play my golden oldies like the Iron Butterfly belting out 'In-A-Gadda-Da-Vida,' he leaves the room."

" 'In-A-Gadda-Da-Whoozis' is a golden oldie?"

"All he likes is bubble-gum music. He sits there shrieking, 'Awss,' which, I take it, means 'awesome.' And he thinks 'far out' is a NASA term. Half the time, I haven't the faintest idea what he's talking about."

"I know what you're going through, believe me," I said cheerfully.

Reuben sighed. "But the very worst was when they had Costumes-from-the-Past Day at his school. I suggested he go as a cowboy, but, no, he insisted on borrowing my old fringed suede jacket, my authentic leather headband, and my genuine Miwuk beads."

"He went as a native American from times of yore?" I asked.

"No, he went as a hippie from times of yore. Costumes of the past indeed! Oh, there's nothing more depressing than when your children reject all you believe in and relegate you to the ash bin of history."

"There, there, Reuben," I said, patting him on the shoulder, "it couldn't happen to a more deserving generation."

So we may, indeed, have become more like our kids once were, but they, in the natural order of things, have retaliated by becoming what we once were. So I say the Generation Gap still exists just as it has always existed and always will exist as long as there are generations. And the way I look at it, you may as well enjoy it. I certainly did my best to enjoy it when I caught Mordred moping through the paper at the breakfast table.

"What's the matter now, Mordred?" I inquired with the usual parental concern.

"You've saddled me with a national debt of one-and-a-half trillion dollars," he said. "That's what's the matter."

"That's quite true," I said, "and I can see why you might be slightly annoyed. But you're young, Mordred. Think of all you've got to look forward to."

"Yeah," he said. "I can look forward to working for forty years to support old guys like you who thought up this Social Security scam. And when I get to the payoff, the cupboard's going to be bare."

"You've got to get into these pyramid schemes early, Mordred. You should have signed up in 1940."

"And how do you feel about running up the biggest foreign trade imbalance in history?"

"Sound as a dollar," I said. "And speaking of sound dollars, let me say your mother and I had a great time in Europe last summer. Imagine a gourmet dinner in Paris for twenty bucks including wine!"

"Swell. And thanks to your profligate spending on yourselves, the entire international monetary system may well belly up at any minute."

"You're being too pessimistic, Mordred. I've calculated the risk carefully, and I'm confident it will hold together just long enough for me to retire in peace to my earthworm farm."

"It's not only my money you've squandered," said Mordred, his voice rising, "it's my natural assets. How do you get off burning up all my fossil fuels?"

I was becoming irritated. "They are not *your* fossil fuels, Mordred," I told him. "They are *my* fossil fuels. Go find your own fossil fuels to squander."

By now, Mordred's lower lip protruded a good quarter inch beyond his upper. "And I suppose you're going to tell me that you haven't carelessly mucked up my environment?"

"Play your cards right, son," I said, "and some day all my toxic dumps will be yours."

"Not to mention your oil spills and your undrinkable streams and the nonbiodegradable plastic you've scattered all over the landscape," he said. "I suppose you expect me to clean up after you?"

"No," I said, "not seeing the way you cleaned up your room."

"What am I supposed to do with the deadly nuclear wastes you've left me because you selfishly created them without bothering to figure out what to do with them?"

"Think of them as heirlooms," I said. "The time will come when they will have been in the family for 250,000 years."

He shook his head sullenly. "Your carbon dioxide is creating a greenhouse effect that is melting my polar ice caps; your fluorocarbons from your spray cans are destroying my ozone layer; because of your prejudices, I have to deal with racism; because of your bumbling, I'm faced with a population explosion; you want to clutter up my heavens, which once twinkled so innocently, with your killer satellites; in fact, it looks as though you may very well get me blown up in your stupid cold war. What on earth have you got to say for yourself?"

I had the answer to that in a split second: "Don't tell me your problems," I said.

He sighed. "I'd feel better," he said, "if you'd just tell me how you plan to pay back these quarter-trillion-dollar deficits you're running up every year to finance your high living."

For the first time, I smiled at him. "I don't," I said.

And I think I speak in all this for my generation. When we were young my generation was seriously split in its ideology. Some young firebrand liberals wanted to soak the rich; and some young respectable conservatives wanted to soak the poor. But now, as we approach our golden years, we are all at last united in our mature wisdom under the same philosophical banner: Soak the unborn!

But I must admit to an occasional twinge of guilt, and for the benefit of my generation, I ask permission to recount a dream I had. The young will find it not as sweeping as Martin Luther King's, but I trust it will give some pleasure to members of my age group.

It was the night of my talk with Mordred. I had gone to bed feeling I might be in for a bit of divine wrath for my sins, and I was therefore somewhat shaken to seemingly awaken several hours later and find an angel at the foot of my bed writing in a golden book.

"Can I help you?" I asked nervously.

"I have come," said the angel, "to grant you one wish."

"Me?" I said with understandable surprise. "A wish? Why me?"

"You have been selected by the Heavenly Computer as typical of your generation," said the angel, "and your generation is to be rewarded for its magnificence."

"There must be some mistake," I said. "We've been downright rotten. We created a racist society . . ."

"Mankind has always been racist," said the angel gently. "You were the first to admit it and attempt a remedy."

"And we militarized our democracy. Why, when I was a boy, we had an army of only 134,000 men."

"You built an army of millions in hopes of bringing

freedom to all the world," said the angel. "Truly, a noble goal."

"Well, maybe," I said. "But you can't deny we polluted the water and the air and scattered our garbage far and wide."

"That is so," said the angel. "But the environment is polluted solely because you constructed the most affluent society the world has ever seen."

"I guess that's right," I said cautiously. "Yet look at the population explosion. Famine and pestilence threaten millions of lives."

"Only because your generation cured diseases, increased the food supply, and thereby lengthened man's life span," said the angel. "A tremendous achievement."

"And our children live in terror of the hydrogen bomb," I said gloomily. "What an awful legacy."

"Only because your generation unlocked the secrets of the atom in its search for wisdom," said the angel. "What a glorious triumph."

"You really think so?" I said, sitting up and smiling tentatively.

"Your motives were excellent, your goals ideal, your energies boundless, and your achievements tremendous," said the angel reading from the Golden Book. "In the eons of mankind, the names of your generation lead all the rest. And therefore, by the authority vested in me, I am empowered to grant you one wish. What shall it be?"

"I wish," I said as the heavenly chosen representative of The Older Generation, "that you'd have a little talk with Mordred."

On the Other Hand . . .

IT WAS A sunny afternoon. Twelve hours earlier, I had become a grandparent for the first time. At the hospital, in these newly relaxed times, I had been allowed to sit on my daughter's bed and hold my granddaughter in my arms. No mask, no gown, no rubber gloves, no thick window to peer through. Just I and my granddaughter to hold and to touch—the way it must have been in the beginning. I came very close to weeping with . . . What? Love, pride, joy, relief, I suppose, and something more.

She was (forgive a grandfather) a beautiful creature—blue eyes, a shock of black hair, and, by some ever-recurring miracle, perfectly formed. As I held that incredibly delicate bundle, I became fascinated with her tiny red feet. I watched her toes constantly curl and uncurl. I had forgotten about newborn infants' feet. If you touch their soles, they will instinctively try to grasp your finger with their toes—a throwback, anthropologists tell us, to the prehensile feet of our tree-dwelling ancestors millions of years ago.

So there we were after millions of years, just the two of us—I, the grandfather, approaching the end of my allotted span (with no great haste, mind you), and she at the very dawn of her own time. Death and life. Sadness and elation. Bang the drum slowly; toll the bells wildly. It was for these things too that I wanted to weep.

For the past several decades, sociologists have delighted in predicting the imminent demise of what they call "the nuclear family." But on that day I never felt more strongly that they were wrong. For the family provides more than love and belonging and security. It provides a sense of continuity, a sense of infinite purpose. I have never been able to believe that we evolved on this tiny planet circling a third-rate sun on the fringes of a mediocre galaxy sailing through a boundless universe only to die on this tiny planet. I believe that the human race has a goal, a purpose, a reason for being—that it is bound somewhere beyond my understanding.

So as my granddaughter's toes grasped for my fingers, I thought of all the millions of years we had come; I thought of my own impending end some day; but, above all, I thought of her fresh beginning, of the millions of years to come to get where we are going.

And that, I deeply believe, is what it's all about.